The Holy Mountains Of The World

Charged In Operation Starlight

Edited by

The Rev. Charles Abrahamson, D.D.

Printed and Published by
THE AETHERIUS SOCIETY
6202 Afton Place, Hollywood, California 90028-8298, U.S.A.

First Published — 1994

THE HOLY MOUNTAINS OF THE WORLD CHARGED IN OPERATION STARLIGHT

ISBN No. 0-937249-14-9
Library of Congress Catalog Card No. 94-070169

The Holy Mountains Of The World — Charged In Operation Starlight is printed and published by The Aetherius Society, 6202 Afton Place, Hollywood, California 90028-8298, U.S.A.

Manufactured in the United States of America.

THE HOLY MOUNTAINS OF THE WORLD
CHARGED IN OPERATION STARLIGHT

Edited by The Rev. Charles Abrahamson, D.D.

By George King, D.Sc., Th.D.

THE NINE FREEDOMS
THE TWELVE BLESSINGS
VISIT TO THE LOGOS OF EARTH
OPERATION SPACE MAGIC — THE COSMIC CONNECTION
OPERATION SPACE POWER — The Solution to the Spiritual Energy Crisis
CONTACT WITH A LORD OF KARMA
YOU TOO CAN HEAL
YOU ARE RESPONSIBLE!
THE THREE SAVIOURS ARE HERE!
THE FIVE TEMPLES OF GOD
THE AGE OF AETHERIUS
OPERATION SUNBEAM — GOD'S MAGIC IN ACTION
WISDOM OF THE PLANETS
LIFE ON THE PLANETS
COSMIC VOICE, VOLUME NO. 1
COSMIC VOICE, VOLUME NO. 2
KARMA AND REINCARNATION
BECOME A BUILDER OF THE NEW AGE
THIS IS THE HOUR OF TRUTH
JOIN YOUR SHIP
A COSMIC MESSAGE OF DIVINE OPPORTUNITY
MY CONTACT WITH THE GREAT WHITE BROTHERHOOD
THE FESTIVAL OF "CARRYING THE LIGHT"
DESTRUCTION OF THE TEMPLE OF DEATH and RESCUE IN SPACE
JESUS COMES AGAIN
THE HEATHER ANGEL STORY
SPACE CONTACT IN SANTA BARBARA
THE ATOMIC MISSION
A SPECIAL ASSIGNMENT
CONTACT YOUR HIGHER SELF THROUGH YOGA
BOOK OF SACRED PRAYERS
THE PRACTICES OF AETHERIUS
THE FLYING SAUCERS
THE TRUTH ABOUT DYNAMIC PRAYER
IMPORTANCE OF COMMEMORATION AND SPIRITUAL HAPPINESS
A SERIES OF LESSONS ON SPIRITUAL SCIENCE ON CASSETTES.

A price catalogue, with complete list of books and cassettes by the same Author, is available upon request.

All books and cassettes by George King, D.Sc., Th.D., are obtainable from the Publishers, The Aetherius Society, American Headquarters, 6202 Afton Place, Hollywood, California 90028-8298, U.S.A., Tel: (213) 465-9652 or 467-HEAL; or from the European Headquarters of The Aetherius Society at 757 Fulham Road, London SW6 5UU, England, Tel: (01) 736-4187 or 731-1094.

DEDICATION

This book is dedicated to His Eminence Sir George King, Primary Terrestrial Mental Channel for Interplanetary Parliament, whose total commitment to the Great Cause of World Peace and Enlightenment gave to mankind the Holy Mountains of the World.

ACKNOWLEDGEMENTS

This book is a **concise** history of the World Mission, OPERATION STARLIGHT. A **complete** history would fill several volumes of this size!

We are deeply indebted to our Master, His Eminence Sir George King, for respecting our judgement in the compilation of this material, while guiding us, at the same time, as to what information should be deleted for valid reasons which were his alone to determine.

Most of all, we gratefully acknowledge the very considerable efforts which he made in establishing Mental Contact with Cosmic Masters to obtain information which would make this book as current as possible.

That our Master chose to expend his priceless time and energy when deeply involved in other Missions of great importance to mankind, indicates his continuing concern that the Truth about OPERATION STARLIGHT be made known!

Cover photograph. This photograph of our Master is one of several which were taken on Mount Ramshead, Australia, by Keith Robertson immediately after the mountain had been Charged. All original negatives show a distinct energy beam flowing from the top of the frame to our Master's head and shoulders.

CONTENTS

ILLUSTRATIONS

PREFACE

The Planet Earth is not our original home! She, an ancient Goddess of immense compassion, Wisdom and Cosmic experience, gave us refuge upon Her surface after we had destroyed Her Brother, the Planet Maldek, through nuclear war. All that remains of Maldek today are thousands of pieces of lifeless rock in orbit between Mars and Jupiter — the Asteroid Belt.

Upon our arrival, the Divine Law required that an ionospheric barrier be erected around Earth. This diminished our access to the Holy Energies flowing from the Sun and other sacred Cosmic Sources. This was not in punishment, but a protection for the grossly involved mental and physical structures of those who had destroyed the body of a Planetary Logos. One immediate effect of this barrier was that it became much more difficult for terrestrial man to contact those subtle forces so necessary for his inspiration and Spiritual evolution.

The Akashic Record shows clearly that we had learned little from our Cosmic crime. Before we could destroy Earth through another nuclear chain-reaction, She was commanded to save Herself! The Planet turned on Her axis and mankind was destroyed instead in the massive floods that swept over Lemuria. We returned, and in our ignorance and evil, again threatened Her life through rampant thermo-nuclear explosion. Again, She turned on Her axis as ordered by The Karmic Lords, and mankind was cleansed from Her surface in the floods which covered Atlantis.

Following each "cleansing," the ionospheric barrier around Earth was further intensified, as required by Divine Law. As humanity began to reincarnate upon Earth for the third time, it had become extremely difficult for humans to contact the Divine Energies. Some made the sublime effort and rose to the Higher Realms. The masses could not — or would not — and our foul history began to repeat itself for the fourth time.

By the year 1945, in the present era, mankind had waged two

world wars. The second had resulted in the deaths of more than 50,000,000 people. On July 16th of that year, the unthinkable reappeared in a gigantic mushroom cloud near Alamagordo, New Mexico. August 6th and August 9th saw atomic bombs dropped, not in test, but again in war by man against his fellow man!

Within seven brief years, the testing of nuclear weapons had escalated until, in 1952, the even more terrible hydrogen bomb became a reality. A race for nuclear supremacy had begun among the major materialistic powers on Earth. Billions lived in daily terror of what appeared to be the inevitable — a third world war of almost certain nuclear devastation of the whole human race.

But worse than this — far worse — the Great Ones saw once more a grave threat to the very life of Earth, Herself.

* * * * * * * *

THE COSMIC MASTERS ACT!

In 1954, Cosmic Intelligences approached George King, a Western Yoga Adept living in London, England, and after he had undergone a period of intense preparation, They appointed him Primary Terrestrial Mental Channel for Interplanetary Parliament. Almost immediately, The Cosmic Masters of our Solar System began giving Transmissions of profound Cosmic Wisdom through Their chosen Channel while he was in positive, Yogic, self-induced Samadhic trance. These Transmissions all pertained to the present dangers facing mankind and the Earth, and urged the people of Earth to turn to selfless Spiritual Service as the only means to prevent the terrible calamity which was facing them.

In addition to these inspiring Messages of Cosmic Wisdom, the Great Masters urged the people of Earth to offer themselves as channels for Spiritual Energies which They would radiate through all cooperators from one of Their own huge Spacecraft, which They called Satellite No. 3, outward to the world as a whole. (Note 1.)

Then the Great Ones went a step further — a truly giant step, as would later be seen — in providing mankind with 19 gigantic sources of Spiritual Energy which could be contacted by active Spiritual workers. These Energies could be radiated through Prayer to the world to uplift, heal and inspire mankind.

The Cosmic Masters directed George King to a series of mountains throughout the globe which he climbed, often under conditions of extreme difficulty, to act as a "terrestrial link" through whom the Masters Charged these mountains as virtual Cosmic Batteries. He was quickly followed by droves of active Spiritual workers who climbed, almost in his footsteps, to contact these Energies and send them outward to the world.

In this way, through a World Mission known as OPERATION STARLIGHT, the Holy Mountains of the world and the selfless Spiritual workers who have prayed from their heights, have helped to offset the effects of the ionospheric barrier around the Planet. Once again, highly potent Spiritual Energies are readily and easily contactable by ordinary people!

This booklet was prepared, not only as a history of OPERATION STARLIGHT, but also as a guide to the Holy Mountains of the world, whose vibrant, uplifting Spiritual Energies await all who would go to these eternal Cosmic Batteries to help bring to the Earth a New Age of enlightenment and peace.

NOTE 1. For information on Satellite No. 3, study of the following Aetherius Society publications is recommended: *The Nine Freedoms,* Chapter 4; *Cosmic Voice, Volume 1,* pages 32-35 and 73-79; *Operation Space Power — The Solution to the Spiritual Energy Crisis.*

CHAPTER 1

HIS EMINENCE SIR GEORGE KING

PRIMARY TERRESTRIAL MENTAL CHANNEL

His Eminence Sir George King was born on January 23rd, 1919, in Wellington, Shropshire, England. His father was a schoolmaster and his mother a noted clairvoyant and Healer. From a very early age, he showed a profound interest in Religion — at that time, orthodox Christianity.

The World War II years were spent in the London Fire Brigade, battling the effects of the Nazi Luftwaffe incendiary and high-explosive raids on London and surrounding areas. During this time he learned personally and deeply of man's inhumanity to man — as well as much about man's capacity for self-sacrifice and bravery.

His interests had turned by this time to the more profound Truths of advanced metaphysics and he became a student of Yoga — practising ever more difficult and challenging Yoga exercises for up to 10 hours daily. His own psychic abilities became very pronounced, including his ability to project into the Higher Realms to pursue his intense search for the highest Truth, with the assistance of advanced intelligences there. By 1954 he was deeply engrossed in Spiritual Healing and had already received advanced Initiations on the Higher Planes.

It was in this year that he received the well-known "Command" to prepare himself to become the voice of Interplanetary Parliament and was soon shown, through a series of highly specialized exercises, how to bring about that elevated state of consciousness absolutely necessary to establish a mental rapport with the Beings Who inhabit the other Planets. He mastered the sciences of Raja, Gnani and Kundalini Yoga until he could consciously attain the state of Samadhi. It was then that The Cosmic Masters of the Solar System began using him as Primary Terrestrial Mental Channel.

Early Transmissions from The Cosmic Masters indicated the wide diversity of Their deep interest in and compassion for mankind. The Master Aetherius from Venus gave a series of simple exercises for mental and physical health which were published as *The Practices Of Aetherius.* This Great Being also announced the beginning of the Magnetization Periods during which a huge Spacecraft, Satellite No. 3, sent powerful Spiritual Energies through all those on Earth who performed acts of selfless Service. The Cosmic Master Mars Sector 6, Who was in control of Satellite No. 3, also delivered many profound Messages, with frequent reference to the terrible dangers of nuclear experimentation. The great Master of Love from Venus, the Master Jesus, also spoke often in words of gentle, yet profound Wisdom to humanity.

Upon the Masters' instructions, His Eminence founded The Aetherius Society in London to help propagate Their Teachings. The Society was extended to the United States, where he became an Ordained Minister. He later earned many degrees, including Doctor of Divinity, and was created an Archbishop in 1980, founding The Aetherius Churches.

At this same time he was recognized by Orders of Chivalry worldwide for his outstanding humanitarian accomplishments and became a Knight of many Orders, and in 1981 was Crowned His Serene Highness Prince George King de Santorini.

To Members of The Aetherius Society throughout the world, His Eminence Sir George King is acknowledged Primary Terrestrial Mental Channel for Interplanetary Parliament and recognized as their Spiritual Master in these latter days before the dawning of a New Age upon Earth!

PRIMARY TERRESTRIAL MENTAL CHANNEL

Primary Terrestrial Mental Channel, His Eminence Sir George King, is a multi-faceted individual of many talents and broad interests. His photographic skills have documented many of the World Missions of The Cosmic Masters. As a part of his deep Spirituality and unconditional commitment to the Divine Plan for World Peace and Enlightenment on Earth, His Eminence is a man of action who knows that practical, selfless Spiritual Action — not detachment and withdrawal from the world and its problems — is the Key to terrestrial salvation.

CHAPTER 2

OPERATION STARLIGHT
A Concise History of the Charging of the Holy Mountains

Phase 1 of Operation Starlight in Great Britain — and the world — took place on a low mountain in North Devonshire, England, called Holdstone Down. The beginnings of this Mission, as was often to prove the case in other Missions given to our Master, was clouded in mystery.

On July 10th, 1958, during a Transmission pertaining to other matters entirely, the Master Aetherius issued a directive to our Master instructing him as follows:

> *"On July 23rd, I want Mental Channel No. 1 in the county of Devonshire.*
>
> *"I want him to go to the crossroads along the lane where he was previously contacted by an Intelligence from Mars. He will go alone. He must not take upon his person any more metal than is absolutely essential. That means he will not be allowed any camera equipment — I am afraid!*
>
> *"He will go to this spot at a time which he will be given just beforehand. When he gets there — he will know why!*
>
> *"I am giving these instructions so that they may be recorded for certain reasons, which you will learn later."*

His Eminence, obeying the instructions of the Master Aetherius to the letter, travelled from London to Combe Martin, a small village in Devonshire, where he carefully reconnoitered the vicinity on July 22nd, to ensure that he would know exactly where to place himself on the following day. He wrote later of some of the thoughts which agitated his mind on this occasion.

"What was the time of the meeting? What was the purpose? Why me? These and about a million and a half other pertinent questions went round and round inside my head like grains of sand in some nightmarish whirlwind. Aetherius — the Infallible ONE — had arranged this coming meeting. Therefore it was to be very important. But when...? How...? Why...? I felt very small indeed during the hours of waiting, before the actual time was given."

The appointed time was given and, when it arrived, His Eminence was at Stoney Cross, a crossroads leading, in one direction, to a narrow path which led to the 1,140-foot summit of Holdstone Down. At Stoney Cross our Master was suddenly contacted by an Adept from Mars Who had previously given him a vitally important Teaching almost on this very spot! This contact consisted of further profound metaphysical information, pertaining mainly to the important position which our Master and The Aetherius Society would occupy as the Cosmic Plan of the Masters for Earth and its people in these latter days was manifested.

At length, the Martian Adept told His Eminence:

"Now, My son, this is your Mission. At the crossroads I will disengage Myself from your consciousness. You will proceed down the other road until you come to a track which leads up to a high place. You will gain this position and will pray for the Power of Peace to be released to the world. ***Pray well, My son, and you will be contacted by One Whose strength has in the past come from those He met upon the hills."***

As His Eminence began to climb Holdstone Down, the meaning of these words dawned upon him and he knew, beyond doubt, the identity of his next Contact! He wrote later of his reaction to this realization:

"A cold perspiration formed in tiny beads upon my

forehead. I took one sweeping and dissatisfied look at my past and wondered why such a Holy Being as He Whom I was due to meet should ever trouble any further with us mere mortals. 'But then,' I thought, 'The very essence of His Mission was to be of sacrifice for Earth.'"

Reaching the summit of HOLDSTONE DOWN, our Master selected a spot looking inland, with a concrete Ordnance Survey pillar at his back, and commenced an audible Prayer for Peace on Earth. Dimly, out of the corner of his eye, His Eminence saw a bright blue sphere of light skip across the night skies. He turned to watch it go far out over the Bristol Channel and then stop to hover dead in its tracks. Our Master turned back and continued his Prayer for suffering humanity. The following are his own words describing, as only he could, a series of amazing events which were the beginning of a new World Mission — ***Operation Starlight!***

THE MASTER JESUS COMES AGAIN!

"A few minutes passed. Then. . . . HE CAME.

"I knew instantly that the God-Man Who stood silently looking down upon me was Jesus.

"What is more, this was no psychic vision, for He was completely physical. He was dressed from the shoulders to the ground in a robe which seemed to glow with a bluish-white incandescence. Beneath the outer garment He wore a tightly fitting undergarment which clung to His tall, lean, rather athletic-looking body as though it were made of a very resilient substance. Around His waist there was a broad, tight band of purple, dotted with jewels, which seemed to live — such was the magnificence of their fire. One large five-pointed jewel in the middle of the front part of the purple belt continually changed colour.

"Fascinated by the radiant beauty, I moved my head slowly upwards and gasped when my eyes lighted upon a really magnificent, pointed, star-like jewel upon His chest. The furthermost points of this living crystal must have stretched from His physical heart on the left hand side, to His Spiritual heart on the right. His outer garment covered these two points, yet I could plainly see the radiations coming through the garment, such was the intensity of the living fire which came from this great, scintillating crystal.

"His face was, to a simple man like me, so wonderful as to be beyond my limited descriptive abilities. His living eyes, clear, bright, shone with the blue flame of the great Cosmic Adept which He is. Such was the light radiated by Jesus that I could plainly see the colour of those eyes. He was, contrary to popular theological belief, clean shaven, with a firm chin, soft, kind lips and a well-shaped nose. His skin was tanned a deep golden colour. I did not see a solitary line upon His broad forehead. His long, light-brown hair fell to His broad, straight shoulders. In His hand He held what appeared to be a short wand, the stem of which seemed to be less than a foot long. This was terminated by a large crystal in the shape of a five-pointed star. I seemed to know without being told that this was symbolic of the Rod of Power from Venus.

"He stood there, silent, unmoving for a short time. Then he slowly levelled the wand in my direction. I tried to rise, but could not move a muscle to unlock my legs from the posture which had been adopted. When the wand was almost level with me, some very gentle urge to extend my arms in front of me seemed to float into my mind. Reluctantly, I turned away from Him and looked out over the dark hills with my arms extended, fingers stiff. Out of the corner of my eye I could see the wand come level. **Then a great surge of vivid blue flame coursed through my body, along the arms and out of the fingertips.** The whole countryside seemed to be swallowed up in a whitish mist as my physical eyes ceased to function. I had to close them.

"I do not know how long I remained thus, for time, as such, was non-existent. All feeling, as registered by the basic senses, had left me. I was not aware of anything save the great streams of Energy which ran through my body like huge waves of vivid blue fire. The physical time of this Transmuting Operation may have been short — a few seconds even — I have no idea. But as abruptly as it started, it stopped. Then I could open my eyes and see Him still standing there — tall, silent, radiant, with the wand held across His chest. He fixed me with a penetrating but kindly gaze for a moment, **then a wide beam of green light sprang out of a faintly luminous shape hovering a few feet above the ground, about 30 yards away.** Jesus moved a few steps to one side, into this beam, and was gone!

"I was alone on the mountaintop, stiff and shivering with cold. I staggered to my feet and looked around. High up in the heavens I saw two bluish spheres of light, like two unblinking stars. They were joined by a third which came **upwards** to meet them. Then these three Spacecraft travelled quickly across the skies to disappear over the western horizon. I knew that He had returned to His own world and my Mission was completed."

Although at that moment His Eminence could scarcely be expected to know it, his Mission had only begun! Two things of magnificence had actually taken place on Holdstone Down. The Spiritual Energies which His Eminence describes above, coursing through his arms and fingertips, were manipulated by Higher Forces to transmute a very dangerous war then brewing in the Lebanon. Second, and infinitely more important to the world as a whole, was that our Master was used to place a tremendous Charge of extremely powerful Spiritual Energy, of frequencies carefully selected for this purpose, into Holdstone Down itself. These made the mountain a virtual Spiritual Power Battery whose Energies were inexhaustible and could be contacted by any ordinary Earth person who went to this mountain to radiate these Energies outward to the world through Prayer!

The Mission thus begun came to be known as **Operation Starlight!**

Source: *Cosmic Voice,* Issue No. 18, October-November 1958. Out of print.

OPERATION STARLIGHT IN GREAT BRITAIN

Holdstone Down, Devon. The Ordnance Survey marker where our Master stood on July 23rd, 1958. The small pile of boulders in the foreground marks where the Master Jesus stood on this historic occasion, which was to be the beginning of Operation Starlight. Here, as in 17 mountainous locations to follow throughout the world, His Eminence served as the Channel for an initial Charge of Spiritual Energy which would make this mountain forever Holy. Thousands of pilgrims have followed him to this spot to radiate this Power to a world locked in a desperate Spiritual Energy crisis.

"THE TWELVE BLESSINGS" ARE GIVEN

Four days later, the Master Jesus began to deliver His Cosmic Concept for the Aquarian Age, "The Twelve Blessings," through His Eminence. These Blessings and Prayers were to become the sacred ritual of choice recommended by The Cosmic Masters for ordinary humanity to use on the Holy Mountains of the world in order to help their fellow man.

"The Twelve Blessings" were delivered through our Master between July 27th and October 12th, 1958. His Eminence received these incredible Transmissions while in a deep, self-induced, Yogic Samadhic trance and published their first edition in November! Due to the immense strain which this placed upon our Master; the vast importance of "The Twelve Blessings" to the future of mankind and their significance to the future of pilgrimages to the Holy Mountains; further Phases of Operation Starlight were delayed by The Cosmic Masters for four months!

PHASE TWO — ASTONISHING!

If any doubts remained in anyone's mind about the importance and validity of Operation Starlight, Phase 2 in Great Britain should forever erase these. An eternally indelible stamp of approval was placed upon the Mission by the Highest Sources in the Cosmos, forever establishing Operation Starlight as a part of the Cosmic Plan!

Following the delivery of "The Twelve Blessings," His Eminence was instructed by the Master Aetherius to visit the small town of Bodmin in Cornwall. He arrived there on November 20th, 1958, with Peter Lawless, an active supporter, and for two days "tramped through the fog and bog of Bodmin Moor," until being instructed to climb BROWN WILLY, at 1,377 feet, the highest mountain in Cornwall. Climbing to the top alone on Sunday, November 23rd, our Master was again mentally contacted by the same Intelligence from Mars Whom he had met near Holdstone Down during Phase 1.

Obeying the instructions given to the letter, our Master again served as the terrestrial anchor through whom the Great Ones placed an initial Charge of Spiritual Energy into the mountain. After this amazing feat had been completed, His Eminence had an astonishing experience which can only be described in his own words:

> "I was instructed to stand upon a certain rock upon the top of the mountain at 2:30 p.m. precisely.
>
> "This I did. Throwing my arms out in front of me, I faced the warm winter Sun.
>
> "Then I heard it — and froze solid — almost afraid to breathe.
>
> "Had I not known better, I should have said that the great Voice that I heard then **was the Voice of God!** But I knew that the Supreme speaks to we mortals through His Emissaries. Even so, I was transfixed — listening in awe to the VOICE which came from above and in front of me.
>
> "I have recorded THE LORD'S DECLARATION verbatim and now make it public, as I have been commanded to do."

The exact content of "The Lord's Declaration" given to our Master at this time is of such stunning importance that it deserves a Chapter of its own in this book under that title. (See Chapter 3.) Suffice it now to say that a week later, on November 30th, 1958, the Master Aetherius stated that "The Lord's Declaration" had been delivered through Primary Terrestrial Mental Channel to Earth by **a LORD OF KARMA,** making the place forever Holy ground!

Source: *Cosmic Voice,* Issue No. 19, March-April 1959. Out of print.

PHASE THREE — FRIGID CONDITIONS

It was December 10th, 1958, when our Master began to climb BEN HOPE, a 3,040-foot peak in the far north of Scotland. He was accompanied on this Phase by Keith Robertson and Brooke Marvin.

At about the same latitude as Russia's St. Petersburg, Canada's Hudson Bay or Alaska's Aleutian Islands, with barely eight hours of daylight at this time of year, Ben Hope would seriously challenge our Master and his small Team. Further, due to severely constrained finances, their equipment and clothing was seriously inadequate, consisting of inexpensive military surplus boots, coats and light climbing ropes picked up when the location was revealed to His Eminence by The Cosmic Masters.

The Team soon experienced some of the bitter facts about climbing this mountain. With virtually no land between it and the Arctic Circle some 600 miles to the north, it is estimated to be the most exposed of all the Holy Mountains. They climbed through rocks and low growth, without a single valley or tree to shelter them from the elements.

In bitter cold, trudging through deep snow, with visibility reduced to about 15 feet, our Master left his Team behind near the summit and disappeared from sight in the swirling cloud layer to complete the Charge, limping in agonizing pain from an injury to his hip which he had sustained during the arduous, hours-long climb. His Eminence made the descent with his helpers as quickly as his injury would allow. They had but a few days before the next Phase was upon them.

PHASE FOUR — MORE BITTER COLD

Our Master, Keith Robertson and Brooke Marvin next travelled 100 miles to the south of Ben Hope and, still in the Scottish Highlands, arrived at the picturesque winter ski resort of Aviemore on December 13th. Situated in the Caingorm Mountain Range, this was the most remote National Nature Reserve in the British Isles. The area had long been associated with psychic activity, of both a positive and a negative nature.

After more than two hours trek through the Rothiemurchus Forest, the Team found themselves at the entrance to the valley of Lairig Ghru, surrounded by deep snow. They made their way to the Sinclair Memorial Hut, which had been built near the site where two Marine Commandos had died of exposure some years previously. Unfortunately, this hut had been built of stone rather than of wood, and was several degrees colder inside than out. A small primus stove carried by the Team was used to melt snow for drinking water, but was useless to warm the hut. Our Master paced up and down throughout the night in order to keep some semblance of warmth in his chilled body in the sub-zero temperature.

Just after sunrise on December 14th, they left the valley of Lairig Ghru and began to climb toward the summit of CRAIG-AN-LETH-CHAIN at 3,470 feet in the Cairngorm Mountains, about three miles north of Ben MacDhui, the highest peak in this range.

Still poorly clothed and equipped, our Master still in pain from his injured hip, the Team fought its way through deep snow and intense cold, forced to traverse the steep, precipitous slope to the summit where The Cosmic Masters used His Eminence as the terrestrial link to Charge Craig-An-Leth-Chain as the fourth Holy Mountain in the British Isles.

PHASE FIVE — TREACHEROUS

Only 200 miles south, still at the latitude of Moscow and the southern tip of Hudson Bay, with only a few days rest, on December 18th, 1958, our Master led the same Team toward the 2,635-foot summit of OLD MAN, Coniston, in the county of Cumbria. Significantly, the word "Coniston" is believed locally to mean "King's Stone."

The going was laborious, with deep snow — and even worse, the approach was covered with ice! Climbing ropes had to be used frequently throughout as high winds continued to polish the slippery ascent, and visibility was limited to only a few feet! This climb was to be remembered as the most treacherous of all the Phases in the British Isles!

PHASE SIX — ENCOUNTER WITH THE ARMY

Our Master had been allowed a little over two weeks hard-earned rest before his new Mission resumed. On January 4th, 1959, he arrived in the Brecon Beacons of South Wales, containing the 2,906-foot summit of PEN-Y-FAN.

With him were Tom Curtis and Don and Vi Beresford. Slightly better equipped now with a single ice-axe, the Team still faced wintry cold. Travelling from London, they had narrowly escaped a collision with an automobile which had lost control on the icy roads. The Team vehicle was towing a small caravan (house trailer) on this occasion, which made their life a little easier.

On January 5th, the Team reconnoitered the area, which included climbing most of the way up Pen-Y-Fan in conditions not far short of arctic. At 10:00 a.m. on January 6th, accompanied by Tom and Don, our Master once more commenced the climb of Pen-Y-Fan, this time via a different route through an army firing range.

The weather was again windy, wet and cold and, on the final steep approach to the summit, the ice-axe was gratefully employed to cut footholds in the ice and deep snow. Our Master was forced to halt the first attempt at the Charge, due to the presence of army personnel on manoeuvres but, after a short delay, decided to go ahead. Don lowered our Master on a climbing rope over a cliff face to the spot where the Charge was to take place. After the Charge had been completed, the Team descended — roped together for safety down the hazardous slope.

It is worth mentioning that the military personnel expressed amazement that anyone as meagerly equipped as the Team was, should venture into this region in such weather, as they had lost several highly-trained and well-equipped men here in winters past! On this occasion, they were searching for a missing Commando, whose frozen body was discovered the following day.

PHASE SEVEN — MYSTERIOUS FOOTSTEPS

Two days later, on January 8th, His Eminence and his Team of Tom Curtis and the Beresfords, arrived in Betws-Y-Coed near the next objective, the 3,485-foot summit of CARNEDD LLYWELYN in the Cambrian Mountains.

The climb on January 9th was through snow up to six feet deep up a steep slope. After nearly five hours, the Team began ascending a rocky portion which appeared to lead to the summit. Here our Master asked Tom and Don to wait while he went ahead to complete the Charge in the failing daylight. Afterwards, the Team had great difficulty in retracing their footsteps downward as the wind-driven snow had filled their boot prints. As a result, the Team wandered too far to their left and encountered a steep decline where the snow was very deep. Sliding down feet first made the best and safest descent, but necessitated digging one Team member out of a huge snowdrift!

During both the ascent and descent, peculiar circular imprints, in a rough triangular pattern, had been noted in the snow. Our Master stated that he had heard footfalls during the ascent, as though someone were climbing with the Team, and that near the Charged Spot he had heard them distinctly and very close by! Of course, he saw no one. This mountain has had a long and mysterious history in matters relating to the occult and is today, for reasons directly related to this Charge, one of the Holiest places on Earth!

PHASE EIGHT — A DELAY

Immediately following the Charging of Carnedd Llywelyn, our Master headed inland towards the Derbyshire Peak District and the next objective — KINDERSCOUT. En route, on January 10th, the icy roads and a steep hill caused the car and caravan to slide out of control. Fortunately there were no injuries nor any damage, but His Eminence wisely decided to delay the next Phase and return to London.

Returning to Derbyshire with Tom and Fred Curtis, our

Master climbed to the summit of Kinderscout where, at 2,080 feet elevation, the mountain was Charged on January 31st, 1959.

PHASE NINE — AN END IN GREAT BRITAIN

On February 25th, 1959, accompanied by Keith Robertson and Brooke Marvin, again in terribly cold weather but without deep snow or ice, our Master served as the terrestrial anchor for the Charging of YES TOR, a 2,030-foot peak in South Devonshire — not far from Brown Willy.

With this vital, but apparently uneventful Charge, Operation Starlight came to a close in the British Isles. But it was not to end there! Read on....

* * * * * * * * * *

Sources: No accounts of Phases 3 through 9 in the British Isles have ever appeared in printed form due to the tremendous pressures upon our Master to complete Operation Starlight in Great Britain in only seven months, as well as to publish the vital first edition of *The Twelve Blessings.* The accounts above are drawn from lectures given later by our Master, or from the diaries of Keith Robertson and Tom Curtis. All are published here for the first time.

Ben Hope, Scotland. With nothing between him and the Arctic Circle on December 10th, 1958, our Master faced the foulest of weather conditions imaginable. In a blinding storm, with a badly injured hip, he enabled this mountain to be Charged with very special Energies of an unique Initiatory calibre. He and his ill-equipped Team suffered appalling hardship here so that mankind might have yet another potent Cosmic Battery whose great Spiritual Power might be radiated to the world.

Old Man, Cumbria. This mountain was Charged on December 18th, 1958, in a raging blizzard. Keith Robertson uses a climbing rope to pull himself forward through the deep snow and against howling winds — both of which were experienced by the Team on this Phase of Operation Starlight. No lesser a Being than a Lord Of Karma Charged Old Man through our Master, an indication that Operation Starlight was to be a Mission of immense importance to the Planet Earth and Her inhabitants.

Brown Willy, Cornwall. The Positive Rock where, on November 23rd, 1958, Brown Willy was Charged and The Lord's Declaration was given. This Holy Mountain is located in the middle of the treacherous Bodmin Moor and extreme caution is required, especially during rainy weather, in approaching it.

Yes Tor, Devon. Charged on February 25th, 1958, Yes Tor was the ending of Operation Starlight in the British Isles. Overlooking bleak Dartmoor, this Holy Mountain is only about 27 air miles from Brown Willy and, with Holdstone Down, forms a powerful triangulation in south-western England.

OPERATION STARLIGHT EXTENDED TO THE U.S.A.

"You will present yourself in the Americas. You will give Our true Message to the people there. You will not go so much as a convertor, but merely to state Our true case as you know it. ***Operation Starlight will be extended to these countries."***

Such were the direct instructions given to His Eminence by the great Cosmic Master Mars Sector 6, to begin what was to become an arduous journey quite literally around the world!

As usual, the most serious concerns were financial. But sheer determination to carry out the orders of the Master, together with some hard work and planning by cooperative Members in London, made it possible for His Eminence, accompanied by Keith Robertson, to board a freighter and, on June 16th, 1959, to land in New York.

Immediately swept up by a flurry of lectures, our Master crossed the United States and finally arrived in Los Angeles, California, where, on July 12th, 1959, he addressed a hugh Flying Saucer Convention. Meeting Monique and Irene Noppe there, he was able to found an active American Headquarters of The Aetherius Society.

The lectures continued — as much from financial necessity as to spread the true Space Message, for it is important to remember that the Mission was being continued on the proverbial "shoestring." But in the meantime, our Master attentively awaited the next instructions regarding Operation Starlight. They were not long in coming.

PHASE ONE — U.S.A.

MOUNT BALDY, rising to 10,058 feet in the San Antonio Mountain Range, just 50 miles east of Los Angeles, is a famous winter-skiing and summer-hiking area. Our Master, with Keith

Robertson, Monique and Irene Noppe, was able to enjoy a ride on a ski-lift to 7,800 feet, where a ski lodge was located.

From there, on August 9th, 1959, our Master led his Team through a densely timbered pine forest, across a treacherous, crumbling ridge, aptly called "The Devil's Backbone," toward a secondary peak at 9,552 feet, just below the barren main peak of Old Baldy. The air was thin and hot — a far cry from nearly all that had gone before in the British Isles. An amazing panorama presented itself of the huge Mojave Desert to the north and the Pacific Ocean to the west.

Members in England had presented our Master with a Bolex 8mm motion picture camera, which was now employed for the first time on a Holy Mountain to provide a full-colour record of this sacred event for posterity.

The Charge was performed at 4:20 p.m. by none other than Mars Sector 6 Himself — a very special Charge, details of which are given in Chapter 4 entitled "The Cosmic Masters Speak."

News media and public reaction was such that, within a few weeks, our Master was able to lead over 100 perfect strangers on a pilgrimage to the Charged Spot where, without hesitation and with obvious devotion, they all participated in a powerful Service of "The Twelve Blessings" for the benefit of their fellow men throughout the world! These large pilgrimages continued through the summers of 1959 and 1960 as Southern Californians responded in large numbers to the news of a Holy Mountain "in their own backyard!"

PHASE TWO — THE SNOW CROSS

Two more months of meetings and lectures followed before, in San Francisco, His Eminence learned — from the Lord Babaji Himself — the general location of the next Charge.

On October 20th, 1959, with Keith Robertson, Monique and Irene Noppe and Charles Abrahamson, our Master began climbing from the 7,000-foot base elevation of Lake Tahoe in the Sierra Nevada Mountain Range of Northern California. He had picked the tallest peak in the area from a topographical map and led his Team towards the 10,800-foot Freel Peak. About halfway to the summit, they turned back in failing daylight. Our Master decided to "go" with his strong impression the next day to look at the mountains around Fallen Leaf Lake, a tiny, very deep jewel located at Tahoe's southern tip.

One mountain in particular had strong appeal. Postcards of the area showed two massive intersecting crevasses on the eastern face of MOUNT TALLAC which, when filled with snow, formed a gigantic snow cross which was visible for more than 20 miles!

The climb on October 21st, 1959, was again through dense forest under the hot California Sun. Our Master and Keith were still amazed at how high the timberline went in the American mountains. The approach from the Fallen Leaf Lake side brought the Team to a very steep scree face which could only be climbed in several traverses. This led to a high plateau near a pile of huge, almost car-sized boulders, which the Team began to cross. Within minutes, our Master waved the Team to a stop and went on alone. The spot chosen for the Charge was just ahead at 9,735 feet, below Mount Tallac's main summit.

Our Master later motioned the Team forward to the newly Charged Rock where Keith painted the Holy Symbol of the Society, together with the date and our Master's name. The rest of the Team, after a brief Service, stared in awe at the magnificent vistas on all sides — from the nearly sheer 3,000-foot drop from the Charged Spot to Fallen Leaf Lake, and out over the huge and majestic Lake Tahoe.

Daylight was fading and storm clouds were gathering as the Team left the Charged Rock to finish the descent in a light rain. They were shortly to learn through His Eminence that the Master Jesus had Charged Mount Tallac! Again, a special Charge had been placed in the mountain and a Message from the Master Jesus was given. These details are to be found in Chapter 4.

Source: *Cosmic Voice,* Issue No. 22, May-June 1960. In print and available from The Aetherius Society. A complete account from which this brief history was abstracted.

PHASE THREE — OUR MASTER INJURED AGAIN!

Shortly after the Charging of Mount Tallac, our Master headed eastward with Keith Robertson and Monique Noppe for an extended lecture tour. It was in February in New York City that he was instructed by the Master Aetherius to proceed to the Mount Washington district of New Hampshire as soon as possible. With many lecture commitments on the East Coast, it was mid-March before the Team made its way to the designated area. What they found there was some of the most atrocious winter weather imaginable!

Mount Adams, 5,798 feet in the Presidential Mountain Range of the White Mountains, was chosen. Snowfall was so deep that the Team was forced to rent snow shoes and to quickly learn how to use them. By this time, the Team was fairly well equipped for winter mountain climbing, with down jackets and anoraks, snow boots, proper climbing ropes and ice axes. All these and more — most especially, determination and endurance — would be needed for what lay before them.

The ascent began on March 15th, 1960. The Team had been recording their activities with a new, recently purchased 16mm Bolex motion picture camera. One scene caught by Keith will be indelibly branded upon the memory of all who have witnessed it. Struggling in snow up to 20 feet in depth, our Master fell, again severely injuring the hip which he had damaged on Phase Three in Great Britain. Helped back to the path by a rope quickly thrown by Monique, our Master continued the climb. Keith Robertson later wrote of this moment:

> "It is extremely difficult to portray human suffering in words, especially when one is writing about someone else's agony. **However, judging by the expression appearing on**

his face at each step he took, the continual biting of the lower lip, the pallid expression appearing with beads of perspiration on his forehead, his pain was becoming excruciating. His stops for breath became ever increasing, as he would sink his head into the crook of his arm, drawing in his breath with the hissing sound that one makes when physical torment is manifesting."

As incredible as it may seem, our Master struggled onward for nearly six more hours, each step more agonizing than the last! A small mountain hut where the Team had hoped to rest was found buried in the snow and useless to them. They pushed on. At last, when it appeared that even his amazing endurance was almost at an end, our Master was used as Terrestrial Channel for Mount Adams to be Charged. He wrote later of that moment — his understatement apparent:

"After an extremely difficult climb on Mount Adams, as described by Keith Robertson, and while still some way below the actual summit, the Great Masters took compassion upon me. I was told that I was not expected to go any further — to suffer any more.

"I asked the Team to wait while I went on ahead. I eventually slumped down in the soft, deep snow and prepared myself as best I could for the Charge to be sent through me into this mountain.

"It came.

"A tremendous surge of terrific Energy went deep into the great mass of that mountain, making it forever — a Holy Place. I felt the very mountain vibrate beneath me. The Charge was manipulated by that mighty Cosmic Master — Mars Sector 6."

The Team descended slowly, arriving at their car after **twelve hours on snow shoes!**

Mars Sector 6 relayed a Message to our Master after the Charge, to be given to the world. This Message appears in Chapter 4, with a description of the special Energies of the Charge.

Source: *Cosmic Voice,* Issue No. 23, November-December 1960. In print, available from The Aetherius Society. A **complete** account, from which this brief history was abstracted.

PHASE FOUR — A HOLY RETREAT

Having been informed that Denver, Colorado, would be the assembly point for the last Phase of Operation Starlight in America, our Master arranged a series of 14 lectures to carry him there from New York City. The Team, still consisting of His Eminence, Monique Noppe and Keith Robertson, had scarcely checked into a Denver motel on April 25th, 1960, when our Master was alerted for a Special Transmission from the Master Aetherius, which stated in part:

> *"I suggest that, in order to successfully complete Operation Starlight in the Americas, you proceed to a very small place — a place which, at the moment, is insignificant to some extent but will not always be so. I refer to the village called — Aspen."* (See Footnote on page 42.)

Our Master immediately contacted Edna Spencer, the Detroit Branch Organizer, as well as Irene Noppe and Charles Abrahamson in Los Angeles, inviting them to become Team Members for the upcoming Phase — an invitation eagerly accepted by all! By April 27th, 1960, the Team of six were on their way from Denver to Aspen in the faithful old Ford station wagon in which our Master had travelled so many thousands of miles across the United States. After making an unsuccessful run up the 11,900-foot Loveland Pass, the tiring Ford was turned back to a garage at the base of the pass.

A mechanic cleaned the air filter of oil, adjusted the carburetor for the unaccustomed high altitude, and the now snarling Ford sailed over the Continental Divide and, on April 28th, carried the Team into Aspen, at 8,000 feet elevation, beneath the towering Rocky Mountains.

The following morning, April 29th, the Team held a practice

climb up Aspen Mountain to accustom themselves to exertion at high altitude. Returning to Aspen, the Team contacted Stewart Mace regarding the rental of Husky dog teams. Due to the season this was impossible, but Stewart agreed to guide the Team if needed, since the entire area was very familiar to him from years of guiding fishermen, climbers and motion picture film crews.

April 30th was spent in checking off equipment — all Team Members now being fully equipped, including ice axes, ropes and crampons — in preparation for climbing their objective, which they now knew to be CASTLE PEAK, 14,259 feet high and a mile and a quarter above their present elevation!

The following day, May 1st, the Team picked up Stewart Mace who would guide them to a high mountain chalet at 11,000 feet, where they would spend the night, arriving there about noon.

Leaving the snowbound chalet at 6:00 a.m. on May 2nd, 1960, the Team followed Stewart a few hundred yards to the throat of the Montezuma Valley. There, Stewart pointed out the route and compared it with the Team's topo map. Then he left to return home. The Team was definitely on its own — "high and dry," so to speak, in an unfamiliar but starkly beautiful, snowy wasteland, surrounded by lofty and majestic peaks still towering more than 3,000 feet over their heads.

It was definitely hard going. The thin air made the climb a breathless, plodding, step-by-step advance. The brilliant Sun reflecting on the omnipresent pure-white snow, was blinding. Worse, it cut through the thin protection of the Team's high altitude facial cream and began — unnoticed at first — to burn their skins.

About halfway to the summit, in "Camilla's Garden," our Master began to realize that he was suffering from severe altitude sickness, with a headache which grew worse with each foot gained.

Climbing a final steep slope, with loose scree beneath the snow, the Team roped together for safety against avalanche and gained the ridgetop leading to the peak. There our Master left the Team and went on ahead for the Charge on a secondary peak, just below the main summit of Castle Peak. Our Master, who had always noted that a great surge of Energy had come to him on the last lap of a climb, now noted its absence. He later wrote:

"Where was the Energy I needed?

"For the first time while performing Operation Starlight, I really prayed desperately for sufficient strength to reach that rock so near and yet, in my weakened condition, so far away.

"After what seemed an age of pain and exertion, I reached the place, only to find that the rock, shaped like an ancient battlement, seemed to be three feet from the ground. Three feet, mind you, and it took every ounce of my strength to pull myself onto it!

"Somehow I managed to control my physical exhaustion and mental turbulence to such an extent that I could perform the manipulations necessary to enable me to act as a Channel for the great Cosmic Power to be sent into this mountain.

"The Power came!

"Castle Peak, 14,259 feet, was Charged by the great Cosmic Masters at 2:30 p.m. on Monday, May 2nd, 1960; a day I shall never forget — a day which, sooner or later, **the whole world will remember!"**

Our Master, still "delirious and physically sick," staggered down to his waiting Team who, seeing that he was barely able to walk, roped themselves to him and, supporting him under both shoulders, began the descent down the treacherously loose scree slope. By this time, dark storm clouds had formed over the mountain, in contrast to the rest of the day, which had been clear and agonizingly bright. Our Master later wrote of what occurred next:

"We struggled down for quite some way until, beyond the Montezuma Mine, I staggered and fell for the last time.

I have never wanted to sleep more before in my life. **But at the same time, I have never realized the importance of my Mission so much.** Suddenly, as though uplifted by the very Power of God Itself — a great strength came to me."

Readers should know that the Team was still at over 13,000 feet elevation — 2,000 feet above and well over a mile distant from the nearest shelter of the chalet in the timberline.

"The Energy had come — Oh, thank God, the Energy had come!

"I pulled myself to my feet, threw off the rope attached to my waist and began my descent alone. As I went further down, the throbbing in my head got less and less until it went altogether. It was as though some strange miracle had happened and the Team told me afterwards that they, too, were amazed by this sudden recovery. Down, down I went across the great ice fields, down the precipitous slopes, sometimes tramping, sometimes sliding toward the chalet.

"It was after my recovery that the other members of the Team began to feel **how really exhausted they were.** But like the people of courage and determination that they are, they plodded on downwards. I would not have blamed any one of them if they had thrown away their heavy packs — but they did not do so.

"It was then that another 'miracle' happened on Castle Peak.

"Monique and Irene Noppe and Charles Abrahamson, who were behind Keith and myself, **were followed down the mountain by a great grey wall of swirling snow blizzard.** It hovered behind them like some great grey monster — as though it were watching and **waiting patiently** for them to reach the chalet before it came down. This is exactly what did happen. **No sooner were we all in the protective warmth of the chalet than the snow blizzard hit with a blinding fury! Great swirling snowflakes reduced the visibility to a few feet in a matter of seconds!**

"The next morning we could not recognize ourselves! The Sun had taken its toll! **Everyone was suffering with terrible second degree burns; lips swollen, noses swollen, with the tight skin glossy under the strain of the swellings."**

The Team trekked slowly back to Aspen on May 3rd, where some of them required medical attention due to the severity of their sunburn. Then, on May 6th, the Team went its separate ways and our Master boarded a plane in Denver alone on May 7th for a flight to London.

On May 14th, 1960, in the Headquarters of The Aetherius Society in London, His Eminence was overshadowed by Saint Goo-Ling, a prominent Member of The Great White Brotherhood. His Message, in part a Commendation to Team Members, appears in Chapter 4. A portion of this Message must be given here, however, to complete the history of Operation Starlight in the Americas.

Saint Goo-Ling, the great Master, over 2,000 years old and still living on Earth in a physical body, declared that:

THE GREAT WHITE BROTHERHOOD HAD MOVED INTO CASTLE PEAK TO USE THIS MOUNTAIN AS A HOLY RETREAT.

Operation Starlight, the most important single occult task ever undertaken on this Earth for the last 100,000 years, was now finished in the Americas, but was far from finished in the world.

Source: *Cosmic Voice,* Issue No. 23, November-December 1960. Still in print and available from The Aetherius Society. A full account from which this brief history was abstracted.

FOOTNOTE: The Master Aetherius was, of course, absolutely correct in His prophesy. Aspen, Colorado, has become world-famous in many respects! It is the centre of the Aspen-Snowmass-Vail-Crested Butte winter sports region. A world-class summer music festival draws performers and audiences from around the globe. Its real estate is among the most sought-after and valuable anywhere. Aspen is the residence of numerous notables, from famous authors and singers to Nobel Laureates!

OPERATION STARLIGHT IN THE U.S.A.

Castle Peak, Colorado. At nearly 14,000 feet elevation in the Rocky Mountains, our Master points the way for the Team's approach to the Castle Peak summit on May 2nd, 1960. The entire Team suffered from severe sunburn and oxygen depletion at this high altitude. His Eminence particularly found this to be an exhausting Charge, since a surge of energy which normally came to him near a summit was not forthcoming until after the Charge had been completed.

Castle Peak, Colorado. Nearing the 14,500-foot summit, our exhausted Master forces himself forward with a tremendous effort of will — with massing storm clouds above presenting yet another threat to the successful and safe Charging of this towering peak.

Mount Tallac, California. Charged on October 21st, 1959, by the Master Jesus, Mount Tallac only displays its famous Snow Cross after very heavy snowfall, which had been lacking in Northern California for seven years before this photo was taken in 1993. This Holy Mountain is on the shore of Lake Tahoe.

OPERATION EXTENDED TO AUSTRALIA

Following the completion of Operation Starlight in the United States, our Master had flown alone to England. On May 17th, 1960, he was on Holdstone Down, North Devon, where the Operation had begun only 22 months previously. At midnight he had a physical contact with a Space Intelligence Who instructed him that Operation Starlight would be further extended in the following sequence:

A. Two mountains to be Charged in Australia.
B. One mountain to be Charged in New Zealand.
C. One mountain to be Charged in Africa.
D. Two countries in Europe to be visited.

These instructions must have been, if anything, even more staggering to His Eminence than the extension of the Mission to America — from a financial point of view alone! But considering that already Operation Starlight had made it possible for Great White Brotherhood Retreats to be moved from the remote Himalayas to Ben MacDhui in the Cairngorm Mountains of Scotland, and Castle Peak in the U.S. Rocky Mountains, our Master and Members of The Aetherius Society leapt to the challenge without hesitation.

PHASE ONE — FOUL WEATHER AGAIN

Flying from Los Angeles, His Eminence and Keith Robertson arrived in Sydney, Australia, on November 10th, 1960, and immediately embarked upon a whirlwind tour of radio and television interviews, as well as public lectures, from Sydney to Melbourne on the south-eastern corner of this vast island continent.

Ron and Audrey Chambers, active Aetherius Society Members, had offered their home near Sydney as accommodation for our Master and Keith. On December 5th, 1960, the four had driven in driving rain to the foot of MOUNT KOSCIUSKO in the Snowy Mountain Range, which His Eminence strongly felt would be the location of the next Charge. Despite the foul weather, the Team decided to make a practice climb up Mount Kosciusko and, nearing the summit, they were suddenly engulfed in a sea of dense mist.

With the 16mm motion picture camera churning, the Team climbed onward, soon encountering rugged terrain in very limited visibility, strong winds and miserable cold. It soon became apparent that the "practice climb" was turning into the real thing, as our Master surged ahead, seemingly oblivious to the difficulties.

By 3:30 p.m. the Team reached a large rock formation where their Leader told them to wait while he went ahead. Keith wrote later:

> "By this time the wind was really howling as we stamped up and down in an effort to remain reasonably warm. At the same time, we wondered about our Leader lost in the misty sea of Meditation and what was happening out there some yards away on that lonely rock, where a chilled body and aching fingers are put in their place as no more than an illusion and one faces the **Reality of Eternity of That Which Speaks.** The thought uppermost in my mind was which great Intelligence would use him as a Channel for the mighty Power to flow into this rocky landscape, making it forever a Holy Place to be held in the deepest reverence. Fifteen minutes ticked by, then suddenly our Master appeared again over the rocks, waving us to come ahead.
>
> **"Mount Kosciusko, 7,314 feet in the Snowy Mountains of New South Wales, had been Charged!"**

Keith's musings, in hindsight, can be seen to be quite prophetic. Immediately after the Charge had been completed through him into Mount Kosciusko, our Master received a telepathic Message from the Master Aetherius to give to mankind. This Message is found in the special Chapter 4, which has been reserved for such information.

The Team performed a Service of "The Twelve Blessings" upon the Charged Spot and, just as they were preparing to leave this Holy site, the weather changed abruptly! The clouds and mist disappeared almost magically and the Team was treated to a magnificent sunset. They retreated to their car and motel in the valley below to await instructions concerning the second mountain which would be Charged in Australia.

PHASE TWO — THE POINTING ROCK

The wait was a short one. The following morning the Master Aetherius contacted His Eminence with instructions and, within two hours, the Team was on its way to the next objective — another mountain in the Snowy Mountains but situated on the opposite side of the Range.

What a difference from the previous Charge! From the village of Thredbo, a ski-lift ran directly to the top of the Ramshead Range, where MOUNT RAMSHEAD, rising to 7,197 feet, was to be Charged! The weather was perfect, and the scenery was among the most lovely the Team had yet seen in Australia. Keith happily wrote:

> "As on Kosciusko, patches of snow lay everywhere, but unlike Kosciusko, the weather was grand, the blue sky dotted with puffy white clouds. The Sun shone down with a warm kindness as we started our trek across the barren, rocky, yet beautiful countryside. The climb was gentle and perhaps can be counted as among the most pleasant Phases of Operation Starlight yet performed."

The summit was reached easily and, after a short rest, our Master prepared to go off to perform the Charge. Taking 16mm motion pictures of his departure, the Team was astonished to note a unique experience. For the very first time in the whole of Operation Starlight, His Eminence was plainly visible during the whole of the Charge, a mere 100 yards distant.

The Charge on Mount Ramshead took place at 1:30 p.m. on

Thursday, December 8th, 1960, and concluded Operation Starlight in Australia.

It is undoubtedly significant that the distance between the summits of the two Holy Mountains in Australia is a mere five miles! Keith later described another highly interesting phenomenon:

> "The terrain on Ramshead bears a remarkable similarity to the terrain of Bodmin Moor in Cornwall, England, where Brown Willy was Charged — except, of course, Ramshead is on a slightly grander scale and more scenic. Even more fascinating is another similarity — **that of the pointing Rock!**
>
> "Throughout the Bodmin Moor region, many examples of pointed-shaped rocks (usually indicating some sacred place) may be seen, perfectly balanced upon other rocks. Quite a number of such rocks can be seen around Brown Willy pointing to St. Michael's Mount, believed by some to be the site of the first Christian Church in the British Isles! One such **identical** type of rock formation is situated a few yards from the now Holy Rock on Mount Ramshead, Australia. It points directly to the Holy Rock itself!"

The Team left the mountain shortly to make preparations for the next Phase which, according to their instruction, would take them some 1,200 miles across the Tasman Sea to another, utterly different land.

Immediately following the Charging Operation on Mount Ramshead, our Master received a communication from Mars Sector 6 which can be studied in Chapter 4.

OPERATION STARLIGHT EXTENDED TO NEW ZEALAND

On December 20th, 1960, upon arriving at the airport to fly

to New Zealand, our Master was pleasantly surprised to find a film crew from the Australian Government Television Station awaiting him, with cameras and lights all set up for a final **short** interview. A full magazine of film was used up, however, before he and Keith could get away.

Arriving in Christchurch on the South Island, some difficulty was experienced, due to the Christmas season, in hiring a necessary car. They were successful, but arriving 220 miles later at the "Hermitage," at the foot of New Zealand's famed Mount Cook, the season posed yet another problem. This famous inn, renowned for its majestic scenery and excellent food, was fully booked, with a large waiting list, except for one night — entirely inadequate for the Team's needs. The next day a last-minute cancellation provided the Team with accommodation through the entire Christmas period — one of those strange things that happens from time to time when great Spiritual Forces are at work!

On December 23rd our Master and Keith made a practice climb of Mount Annette in driving rain, but turned back short of the summit, convinced that this was the wrong peak.

The next day, December 24th, they set out early in the morning for another practice climb, this time on the 6,651-foot MOUNT WAKEFIELD, on the other side of the "Hermitage" and the other side of the giant Tasman Glacier. With no detailed maps of the mountain available, the Team could only estimate the best route up the slopes.

The going was steep and hazardous; glacial action had scoured great valleys and littered them with rocks, which at times proved to be treacherous. Our Master wrote of an incident early in the climb:

> "At one time I tested a large rock and it seemed safe enough, until I put my weight on it, when it slipped from underneath me. I immediately twisted around, fell and slid for a few feet as the **whole floor of the valley moved downwards!** At once, I dug in hard with the ice axe and for one terrible moment, found no purchase for it. There I was on

a valley floor with the whole floor starting to move! I hit down again with the ice axe, managed to wedge it securely between two rocks and hung on. Meanwhile, Keith, who was ahead of me, came back and threw me a rope and pulled me out of danger. I staggered up and carefully took stock of the physical damage done by this heavy fall. The back of my hand was cut and badly bruised, **but the worst was a heavy blow on the right hip which had been hit by a falling rock.**

"When I set off again, I breathed a little Prayer that the hip would not go stiff on me until the job was done, for we were no longer practising. **This was the real thing!**"

AN UNFORGETTABLE CHRISTMAS EVE

Come what may, he was now committed. Knowing this with the same certainty that had enabled him to overcome the agony of Ben Hope, Mount Adams and Castle Peak, our Master climbed on. The higher the Team went, the more dangerous the rock became. The footing gave way again a little farther on, and it took all the strength and skill which His Eminence and Keith could muster to extricate themselves from another hazardous situation.

An unavoidable detour at this point lost them several hundred hard-earned feet of elevation, but they eventually reached safer ground and, after another hour's struggle upward, the Team found itself near the main summit. Our Master wrote later:

"After a few minute's rest, I went on again to the spot which was to be Charged. The time was now 4:00 p.m. and it had taken **six and a half hours of really hard climbing to reach this spot.** In these southern latitudes the days are not very long, so one had to consider this.

"I stood for a moment in silent Prayer, then assumed a sitting position on these large rocks.

"The world with its cares, worries and even happiness, was forgotten. I felt my consciousness soar so that it became all-inclusive by its expansion. It was Christmas Eve and although not really commemorative of His birth, nevertheless it was a time when people turn their thoughts toward Jesus — the Master of Love.

"It came gently at first, did that Power, as though from afar. Then it became stronger, more definite, vibrant. It flowed through me into the cold rock of Wakefield in a stream of multi-hued fire projected from the **Heart of the Master Jesus Himself!** Then He spoke:

"'Oh, My Son, you have done well. The land can now rejoice, for this place is Consecrated by My Blessing.'"

The full text of this Message, a combination of mystical beauty and pure Spiritual practicality, appears in the special Chapter 4, reserved for these Transmissions.

After Keith had painted the Holy Rock in the usual fashion, the Team began a descent using a different route, which they hoped would take them quickly off the mountain. Losing height quickly, they were soon faced with a sheer, impassable precipice. Changing direction, they fought their way through dense, tough brush — only to encounter another precipitous rock wall!

TRAPPED ON THE MOUNTAIN

By this time the Sun was setting and night was coming on fast. Our Master and Keith were faced with a difficult decision. They could not continue downward, yet they could not remain where they were as their supply of water was exhausted. This meant only one thing. In the near dark, they made the long climb back upwards to the only mountain stream they had seen, several hundred feet beneath the Charged Spot!

They had both fallen several times but managed to drag their weary, bruised bodies back across the face of the mountain to the stream, where they decided to rest for the night and tackle the problem of getting down the next day.

They built a tiny fire using nearby brush. This and a warm drink helped to keep the cold out. . . . for a time. Our Master wrote:

> **"It began to rain. . . !**
>
> "The cold, damp air at that altitude, about 6,000 feet, cut through us like a knife. Not only did the rain succeed in putting out our small fire, but had all the heather around us so wet that it was no longer burnable. We shivered in the cold, biting rain on that mountain!
>
> "Throughout the long hours of darkness, Keith and I — lying in our soaked anoraks on the wet grass — took it in turns to rub each other's backs vigorously, in order to stop the cold from doing us lasting harm. The seconds dragged by and became minutes and, after what seemed a lifetime, became hours. It was about one o'clock in the morning when a rather amusing incident took place. Keith Robertson turned to me and said: **'A happy Christmas, George!'**
>
> "After what seemed like an age of shivering, the Sun rose above the mountains, painting the clouds a brilliant red. At last, the dawn had come!"

THE SUFFERING CONTINUES

Our Master and Keith discussed their options, which looked much better in daylight. His Eminence wrote:

> "We decided to climb right back up to the main ledge in order to get over this huge valley which separated us from the part of the mountain that we had climbed up. So lifting our heavy packs onto our aching shoulders, **we climbed Wakefield for the second time!**
>
> "But our suffering was not yet over. I was attacked by a sudden and **unexplainable sickness.** As we climbed, the sickness became worse. As the Sun rose higher, it got hot-

ter. We soon exhausted our meager water supply. The going down was just as dangerous, if not as physically tiring, as the climb up had been. As the day wore on we became more and more thirsty. The mysterious sickness became better as quickly as it had started. As for Keith, he too was faring badly because he had blisters on his feet which were now red-raw and bleeding. It was just as though we were on some desert, miles away from civilization and water. What probably made the whole thing worse was that we could see, a few thousand feet below us, a cold stream of crystal-clear water running from the Tasman Glacier."

The eventual arrival, hours later, back at the "Hermitage," was greeted by a worried staff. A rescue team had been sent out earlier, but had been forced to turn back due to the terrible weather conditions. A beautiful lunch was specially prepared and served for the weary pair in the restaurant. Our Master, unable to eat a bite due to his burned mouth, was only able to gaze hungrily at a truly magnificent lobster salad while drinking many cups of tea!

Arriving back in Los Angeles on December 29th, 1960, our Master was shown proudly around the new Headquarters of The Aetherius Society on Hobart Boulevard by Monique, Irene and Charles. Our Master recalled:

> "We had not celebrated Christmas, but we **did** celebrate the New Year!"

Source: For complete, moving details of the three Phases in Australia and New Zealand, from which the above brief accounts were abstracted, see *Cosmic Voice,* Issue No. 24, May-June 1961. Still in print and available from The Aetherius Society.

AN UNIQUE PHASE IN AFRICA!

Some six months following the Charging of Mount Wakefield in New Zealand and before the next Phases in Europe, His Eminence received information from Saint Goo-Ling, Keeper of the Seal of The Spiritual Hierarchy Of Earth. This great Master, long and closely associated with The Aetherius Society, stated that He had seen fit to personally Charge MOUNT KILIMANJARO on behalf of His Eminence and The Aetherius Society.

On October 5th, 1993, our Master contacted the Master Aetherius regarding Kilimanjaro and was given the information that this remote mountain had been Charged by Saint Goo-Ling and two chosen high-ranking Members of the Supreme Council of The Spiritual Hierarchy Of Earth. It was at this time that His Eminence revealed definitely that Mount Kilimanjaro had long been a very large and important Retreat of The Great White Brotherhood prior to its Charging in 1961!

For reasons given later, it is apparent that the Charging of this mountain was essential to the overall plan of Operation Starlight. Considering the time, its location and its height, it would have posed difficulties and dangers to our Master and his Team which The Cosmic Masters appear to have considered excessive.

Mount Kilimanjaro is 19,335 feet in elevation! Located just inside the border of Tanzania (formerly Tanganika), this famous peak is best approached through Kenya, which in 1961 was just beginning to recover from years of Mau Mau uprising and savage war between Kenyan natives and European settlers and visitors. To pass through Kenya en route to Tanzania at that time would have been extremely hazardous!

OPERATION STARLIGHT IN AUSTRALASIA

Mount Ramshead, Australia. Located in New South Wales, the peak of this mountain is only a few miles from Mount Kosciusko, which was Charged on December 5th, 1960. Mount Ramshead was Charged through our Master on December 8th. Note the interesting phenomenon over His Eminence's head. This is on the negative!

Mount Wakefield, New Zealand. This Mountain was Charged on Christmas Eve, 1960, through our Master who was trapped, with Keith Robertson, overnight high on its austere slopes, in driving rain and wind. A rescue team dispatched on Christmas morning was turned back by the bad weather.

OPERATION STARLIGHT EXTENDED TO EUROPE

A gap of seven-and-a-half months occurred between the Charging of Mount Wakefield in New Zealand and the next Phase in Europe. Lest anyone believe our Master had been idle during this period, consider the following:

1. Between February 12th and March 15th, 1961, His Eminence received a series of Transmissions from Mars Sector 6 called "The Nine Freedoms." These astounding Teachings are a guide for all men from the Karmic confines of Earth through glorious Ascension into the lasting Freedom of Interplanetary and Solar Existence. This mystic text was published and is available from The Aetherius Society.
2. Attended and addressed a highly successful Flying Saucer Convention in Los Angeles.
3. Received four additional important Cosmic Transmissions.
4. Gave a series of nine public lectures in depth on "The Nine Freedoms" Transmissions at the American Headquarters.

Leaving Los Angeles in the summer of 1961 with Monique Noppe and Keith Robertson, our Master flew to London where, at the European Headquarters, he began to prepare a Team of seven additional young Members, six of whom were without mountain-climbing experience, for the European Phases.

This Team of 10, the largest and best equipped ever in Operation Starlight, left England on August 4th, crossing the English Channel by ferry to Dunkerque, camping out overnight some 60 miles north at Arras, in what was to become a nightly feature of their stay on the Continent. Two purposes were served in this way: the Team conserved their slender financial resources, and the bulk of the Team gained invaluable experience later to prove **very useful!**

The new Team Members were Ray Nielsen, Reg and Gerry Holdaway, William Mayhew, Neil Goldie and Michael Park.

Our Master decided that Switzerland was almost certainly a likely country, and on August 10th the Team found itself in Davos, where the first practice climb was conducted on a near-by range and most of the Team had its first taste of overnight camping at high altitude. This taste consisted of high winds and pouring rain through a sleepless night!

OPERATION STARLIGHT — SWITZERLAND

On the morning of August 11th, His Eminence informed the Team of instructions he had received from Cosmic Intelligences, that a mountain visible to them miles away across a steep valley was their objective. Study of a map identified the mountain as MADRIGERFLUH, and indicated a likely route for an approach to its distant peak.

Five Team Members were dispatched back to Davos to pick up the rest of the food and equipment which would be necessary for what appeared to be the long and strenuous trek ahead. This move, plus the careful study of their map, proved to be extremely wise in the days to come.

The Team, together again by nightfall, spent another tempestuous evening in driving rain which half-flooded their campsite. Early the next morning, August 12th, still in a downpour which threatened to wash their camp away completely, the Team abandoned its vulnerable site for a move to the Korbshorn Hut, indicated on the map as being some two miles distant along their intended route.

Our Master and Monique left first, shortly followed by Ray, Keith, Bill, Reg and Gerry, with Neil and Michael bringing up the rear. All made the comparative comfort and security of the hut safely, but by noon, the downpour had changed into a raging blizzard! His Eminence, Keith, Bill and Reg left the warmth of the hut and returned to the previous site to retrieve the tents which had been left behind.

Their former campsite had become a veritable lake of ice! The tents were frozen stiff and had to be pried from the icy tundra, to be carried — at least twice their normal weight and still almost fully erected — two miles more through the blinding blizzard to the hut! Fortunately a roaring stove and ample dry fuel awaited them there and, fortified with hot drinks, the four — including our Master — soon recovered from their strenuous exertion and hazardous exposure.

In the hut, the Team took stock. They were reasonably comfortable and secure, with food for five days. All appeared fit for climbing. Photographic and climbing equipment had all survived intact. The weather, still a howling storm outside, seemed to be the biggest factor opposing them.

Sunday, August 13th, 1961, dawned cold, crisp but sunny. The object of their efforts, the mighty Madrigerfluh, towered plainly and clearly above them on the opposite side of the valley.

Our Master decided that, rather than lose the initiative to the elements by waiting, possibly forcing a withdrawal later with nothing accomplished and all their effort wasted, an attempt should be made at once to complete the Phase.

The Team was shortly underway. As they climbed higher, the loose scree underfoot became covered with snow, making the going much easier. A deep gulley, forcing a detour, caused some delay and, by 11:30 a.m., the clouds had begun to amass once more.

At noon the Team had reached a stretch of ground just below the summit where our Master halted them and told them to wait. Alone, he climbed the last few hundred yards to the top and disappeared over the reverse slope, out of the Team's view. A short time later, he reappeared and waved them forward. **Phase 18 of Operation Starlight was now completed!**

Our Master had experienced a severe drop in body temperature, but soon revived. Still and motion pictures were shot and by 4:00 p.m., the Team was back in the hut, returning safely to Davos on August 14th. The next day the Team had to split up. Bill, Reg, Gerry, Ray and Neil were near the end of their annual holidays and had to return to England.

His Eminence, Monique, Keith and Michael remained to complete any further Phase or Phases of Operation Starlight which The Cosmic Masters might call upon our Master to perform. The mighty Mission, begun over three years earlier, was now drawing to a close!

THE FINALE

The much smaller Team of four left Davos on August 16th, 1961, following telepathic instructions to our Master that one more mountain remained to be Charged in Operation Starlight.

Heading westward on a "hunch" that their next objective might be France's Mont Blanc, the highest peak in Europe, the Team arrived in the vicinity of Chamonix on August 19th.

A very significant question was that, although the current Operation Starlight Team could easily manage the climb to Mont Blanc, which takes three to four days through deep snow at the best of times, how many pilgrims would be able to accomplish this later? Would The Cosmic Masters consider this in choosing the next mountain?

Our Master had suddenly become ill and had spent the night in a hotel in Chamonix, but arrived at the Team campsite the next day, his health — which strangely seemed to suffer greatly through this great Karmic manipulation — much improved.

The Team left its campsite on August 21st, 1961, near Les Bossons and took the ski-lift to Bellevue, where they boarded a tramway which carried them up precipitous cliffs to "LE NID D'AIGLE" (The Eagle's Nest), which is the base for a climb of Mont Blanc. They took a long, tedious hike up a steep, rocky slope towards a high peak en route to Mont Blanc, from where they had a better view of what lay ahead. The Mont Blanc summit was still a good two days climb, with the possibility of an overnight stay at a newly-built mountain hut.

Were they to go back and provision themselves for an

attempt the next day on the massif ahead, or would the Charged Rock be somewhere along the ridge just facing them? The latter seemed most likely. Our Master made the decision. The Team would return to Les Bossons and make a climb the next day, fully equipped and provisioned for a possible ascent of the 15,800-foot Mont Blanc!

August 22nd was spent, however, in making local enquiries about climbing conditions in the area and in arranging full climbing equipment for what might prove to be a very difficult effort. These preparations took part of the next morning as well.

By 10:45 a.m. on August 23rd, 1961, His Eminence, with Keith and Michael, had returned to "Le Nid d'Aigle" and set off again up the steep, rocky trail. The weather was fine and, taking photographs and motion picture footage, they clambered over huge boulders and across deep crevasses to the point on the ridge they had reached two days previously. They had come again to a crossroads. Were they to continue on to Mont Blanc, or forge ahead along the ridge overlooking the Chamonix Valley?

Minutes ticked by as our Master pondered the situation. Finally, he decided to strike out along the ridge!

The Team began walking across a snowdrift some 30 feet deep toward a distant heap of brown rocks on the edge of the precipice overlooking the Chamonix Valley. After about 25 minutes of slow trudging, our Master called a halt for a brief lunch, and then decided to set off alone. Anticipating that the spot to be Charged might lie just ahead, he prearranged signals for the waiting Team. If he waved his ice axe, this would indicate that he was on the right track and would then climb the wall of rock. If not, he would beckon them on.

The conclusion, while awaited with baited breath by those present, can hardly be made to seem more than anti-climactic to readers. Keith wrote later of the next few minutes:

> "Hastily picking up the 16mm movie camera, I filmed his departure with mixed feelings — hoping that this rocky

ledge would be the place chosen by Space Intelligences for the Charged Rock.

"Indeed it was!

"Our Master, waving his ice axe at us, suddenly branched off and started to climb the rocky cliff to our left.

"The minutes ticked by. We wondered what was happening, high on that cliff overlooking the peaceful little valley of Chamonix....then suddenly our Master appeared again, waving his ice axe for us to come ahead....

"IT WAS FINISHED! THIS GIGANTIC OPERATION WAS NOW OVER!

"It was hard to grasp at first, yet it was true enough. **After three years of travelling and hardship and suffering, on August 23rd, 1961, Operation Starlight was now over!**

"How long, I wondered, would it take for mankind to realize the vital significance of this gigantic task?

"The Earth is now adorned with nineteen jewels in Her body. One stage further has been completed in the preparation of the wedding gown for the Cosmic Bride. The Earth is now one step nearer to Her great Initiation which **those with a troubled conscience do not look forward to.**

"Will it take a new race of men to appreciate Operation Starlight, which has given to man a key to his Salvation? It is up to man now whether he uses this key, or throws it yet again into the bottomless pit of ignorance. One thing is certain! Next time this happens, it will take place upon a distant Planet, **for those allowed to remain upon this Earth in Her glorious New Age will be those who have taken the key now offered and used it....wisely!"**

Source: Full, detailed accounts from which these two brief reports are abstracted, can be found in *Cosmic Voice,* Issue No. 26, July-August 1962. Still in print and available from The Aetherius Society.

OPERATION STARLIGHT IN EUROPE

Le Nid d'Aigle, France. Our Master rests on the Charged Rock high above the Chamonix Valley on August 23rd, 1961. Just minutes before, a great surge of mighty Spiritual Energy had flowed through him into this peak, bringing Operation Starlight to a highly successful conclusion after 37 months. Nineteen New Age Power Centres had been Charged by The Cosmic Masters throughout the world, 18 of them through His Eminence, who had travelled the entire Western Hemisphere and beyond in the performance of this gigantic task. The fruits from this Cosmic Seed would soon begin to appear in even other World Missions in the years ahead. Our Master would occupy a central position in all of these, and the world as a whole would be the beneficiary as the Cosmic Plan used him to advance its all-embracing cause upon Earth.

Mount Madrigerfluh, Switzerland. Charged on August 13th, 1961 — the day after a fierce blizzard which caught the Team on the slopes — this Holy Mountain was climbed by the largest and best-equipped Team which our Master had yet been able to put into the field in Operation Starlight.

Le Nid d'Aigle, France. The Team works its way cautiously across a snow-covered ridgeline on the way to Le Nid d'Aigle near Mont Blanc, for the final Charge in Operation Starlight which took place on August 23rd, 1961 — three years and one month from its beginning on Holdstone Down.

OPERATION STARLIGHT TEAMS

The Team, Castle Peak. From left to right: Keith Robertson, Irene Noppe, our Master, Edna Spencer and Monique Noppe in a rural Colorado cafe in May of 1960. Not shown is the photographer, Charles Abrahamson.

The Team, Madrigerfluh. From left to right: Reg Holdaway, Bill Mayhew, Monique Noppe, Raymond Nielsen, Neil Goldie and Keith Robertson. Not shown are our Master, Gerry Holdaway, Peter Lawless and Michael Park.

ATTENTION READERS

The next two pages contain an outline of the Charging of the Holy Mountains of the world. You may believe that you have seen this outline before in earlier publications, and might skip over it without careful study.

Restrain that impulse and give these pages your utmost attention!

There are at least seven new entries.

Each of these represents a mental contact with the Master Aetherius or other Cosmic Intelligences. Our Master initiated these contacts — not for his own edification, but in order to obtain permission to tell *you* what, in many cases, *he* already knew.

Carefully studied, these could be the most important pages in this book! Casually read, they will mean little, and you will be the loser!

HOLY MOUNTAINS OF THE WORLD

MOUNTAIN	DATE	CHARGED BY	TEAM
Holdstone Down ***Devon*** ***England***	23 July 1958	The Master Jesus	His Eminence
Brown Willy ***Cornwall*** ***England***	23 Nov. 1958	A Lord Of Karma †	His Eminence Peter Lawless
Ben Hope ***The Highlands*** ***Scotland***	10 Dec. 1958	Mars Sector 8 and close Cosmic Associates	His Eminence K. Robertson B. Marvin
Creag-An-Leth-Chain ***Grampian*** ***Scotland***	14 Dec. 1958	A Lord Of Karma †	His Eminence K. Robertson B. Marvin
The Old Man Of Coniston ***Cumbria*** ***England***	18 Dec. 1958	A Lord Of Karma †	His Eminence K. Robertson B. Marvin
Pen-Y-Fan ***Powys*** ***Wales***	6 Jan. 1959	The Cosmic Adept - The Full Aspect of Nixies Zero Zero Two ††	His Eminence Tom Curtis D. Beresford V. Beresford
Carnedd Llywelyn ***Gwynedd*** ***Wales***	9 Jan. 1959	The Cosmic Adept - The Full Aspect of Nixies Zero Zero One ††	His Eminence Tom Curtis D. Beresford V. Beresford
Kinderscout ***Derbyshire*** ***England***	31 Jan. 1959	Charged by Primary Terrestrial Mental Channel with the guidance and assistance of The Master Aetherius	His Eminence Tom Curtis Fred Curtis
Yes Tor ***Devon*** ***England***	25 Feb. 1959	The Cosmic Adept - The Full Aspect of Nixies Zero Zero Three ††	His Eminence K. Robertson B. Marvin
Mount Baldy ***So. California*** ***U.S.A.***	9 Aug. 1959	Mars Sector 6	His Eminence K. Robertson M. Noppe E. Noppe

MOUNTAIN	DATE	CHARGED BY	TEAM
Mount Tallac *Lake Tahoe* *No. California* *U.S.A.*	21 Oct. 1959	The Master Jesus	His Eminence K. Robertson M. Noppe E. Noppe C. Abrahamson
Mount Adams *New Hampshire* *U.S.A.*	15 March 1960	Mars Sector 6	His Eminence K. Robertson M. Noppe
Castle Peak *Aspen* *Colorado* *U.S.A.*	2 May 1960	The Master Aetherius	His Eminence K. Robertson M. Noppe E. Noppe C. Abrahamson Edna Spencer
Mount Kosciusko *New South Wales* *Australia*	5 Dec. 1960	The Master Aetherius	His Eminence K. Robertson
Mount Ramshead *New South Wales* *Australia*	8 Dec. 1960	Mars Sector 6	His Eminence K. Robertson
Mount Wakefield *South Island* *New Zealand*	24 Dec. 1960	The Master Jesus	His Eminence K. Robertson
Mount Kilimanjaro *Tanzania* *Africa*	July 1961	Saint Goo Ling and two Chosen High-Ranking Members of The Supreme Council of The Spiritual Hierarchy Of Earth	
Mount Madrigerfluh *Switzerland*	13 Aug. 1961	The Master Aetherius	His Eminence K. Robertson M. Noppe Ray Nielsen Reg Holdaway G. Holdaway W. Mayhew P. Lawless N. Goldie M. Park
Le Nid D'Aigle *France*	23 Aug. 1961	Mars Sector 6	His Eminence K. Robertson M. Noppe M. Park

IMPORTANT NOTES ON OUTLINE

† The Lord Of Karma referred to here was *not* the Karmic Lord Mars Sector 6.

†† These great Cosmic Adepts are all Members of the famous Team of The Five Adepts.

The following is a statement made by our Master, His Eminence Sir George King, Primary Terrestrial Mental Channel, just a few days before his approval of this text for publication:

> "In a Mental Transmission to His Eminence on January 8th, 1994, the Master Aetherius made it known that the Cosmic Adepts — the Full Aspects of Nixies Zero Zero Two and Nixies Zero Zero Three — had no choice in the position of the mountains They Charged because, by the Law of Karma, Operation Starlight had to be finished in Britain at that time. These two mountains are not ideally situated."

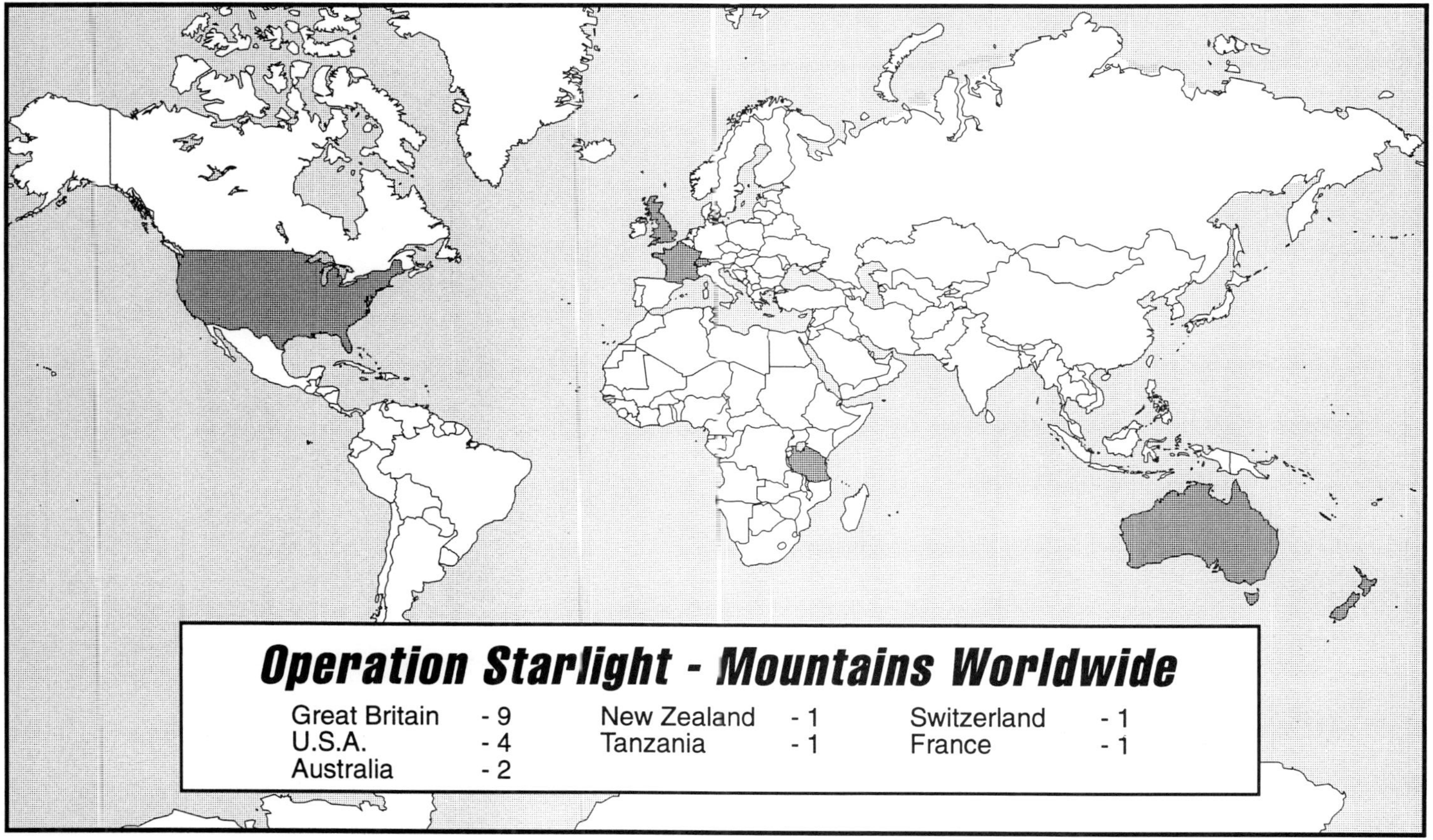
Operation Starlight - Mountains Worldwide
Great Britain - 9
U.S.A. - 4
Australia - 2
New Zealand - 1
Tanzania - 1
Switzerland - 1
France - 1

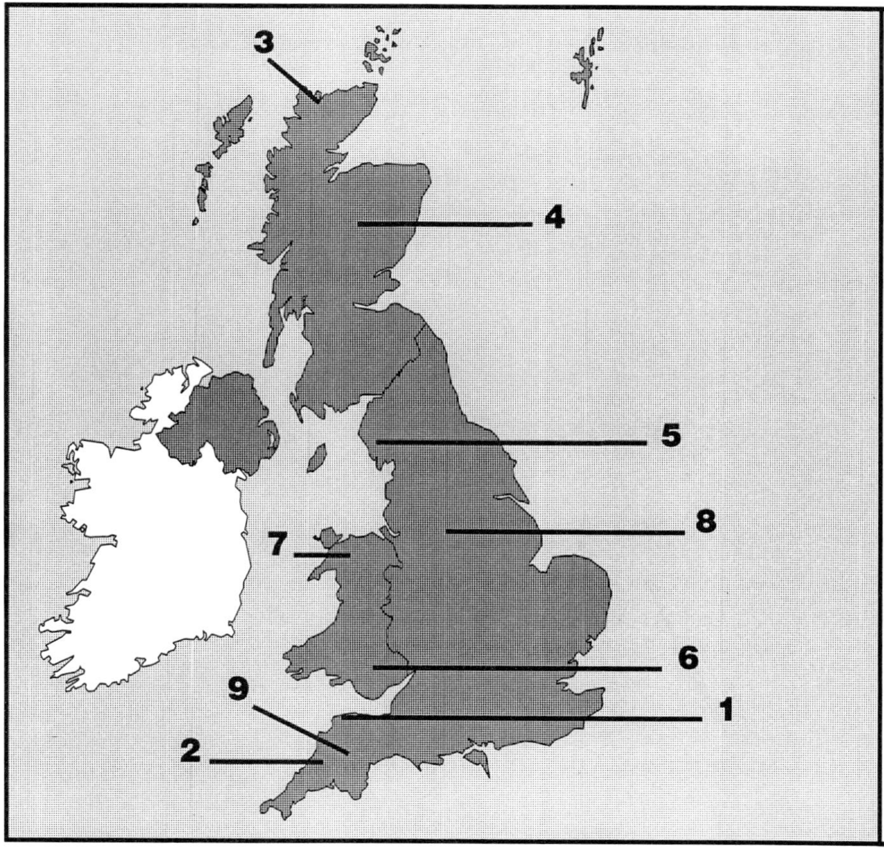

Operation Starlight in the British Isles

1 Holdstone Down

2 Brown Willy

3 Ben Hope

4 Craig-an-leth Chain

5 Old Man

6 Pen-Y-Fan

7 Carnedd Llywellyn — p. 120

8 Kinderscout

9 Yes Tor

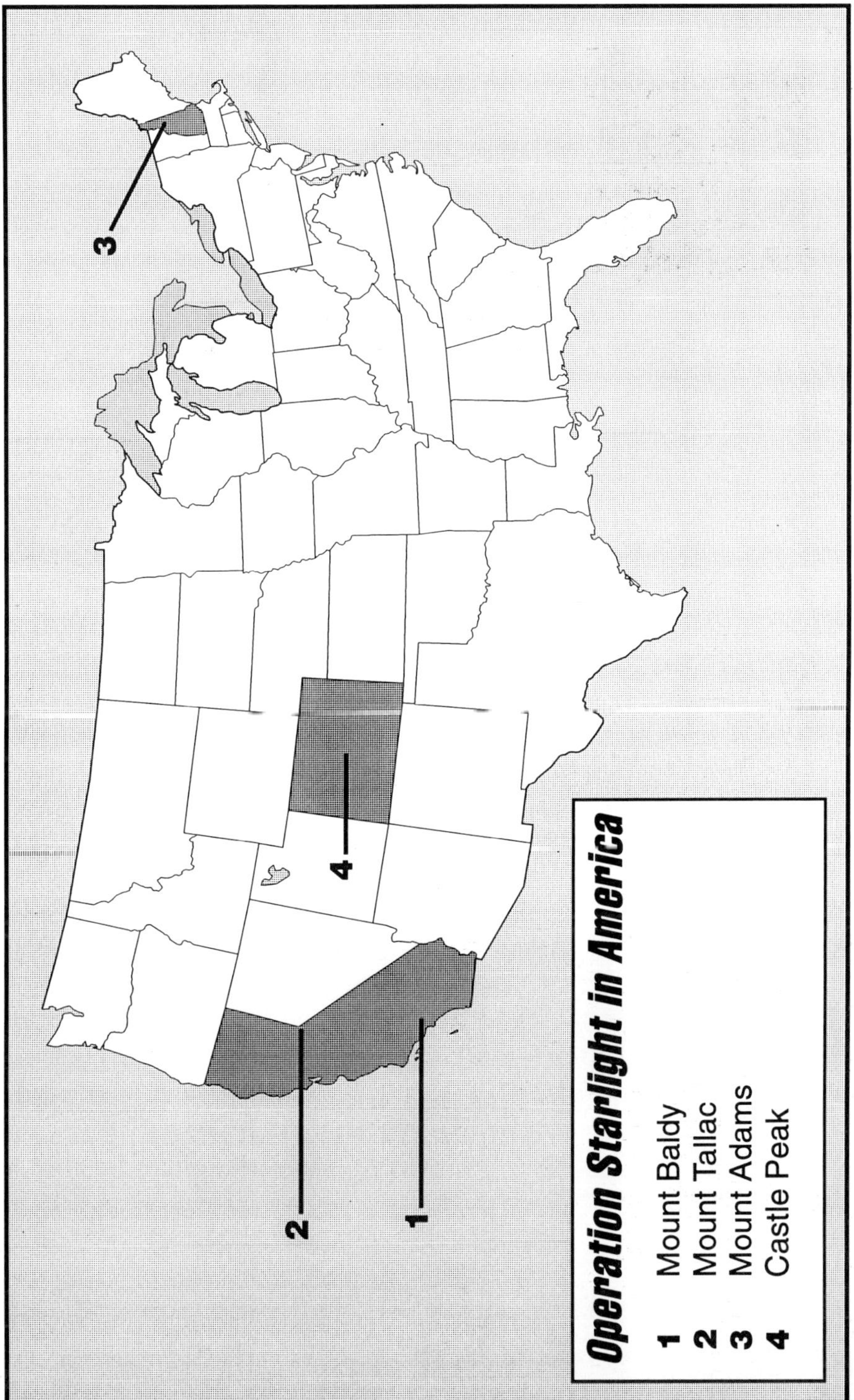

Operation Starlight in America
1 Mount Baldy
2 Mount Tallac
3 Mount Adams
4 Castle Peak
1
2
3
4

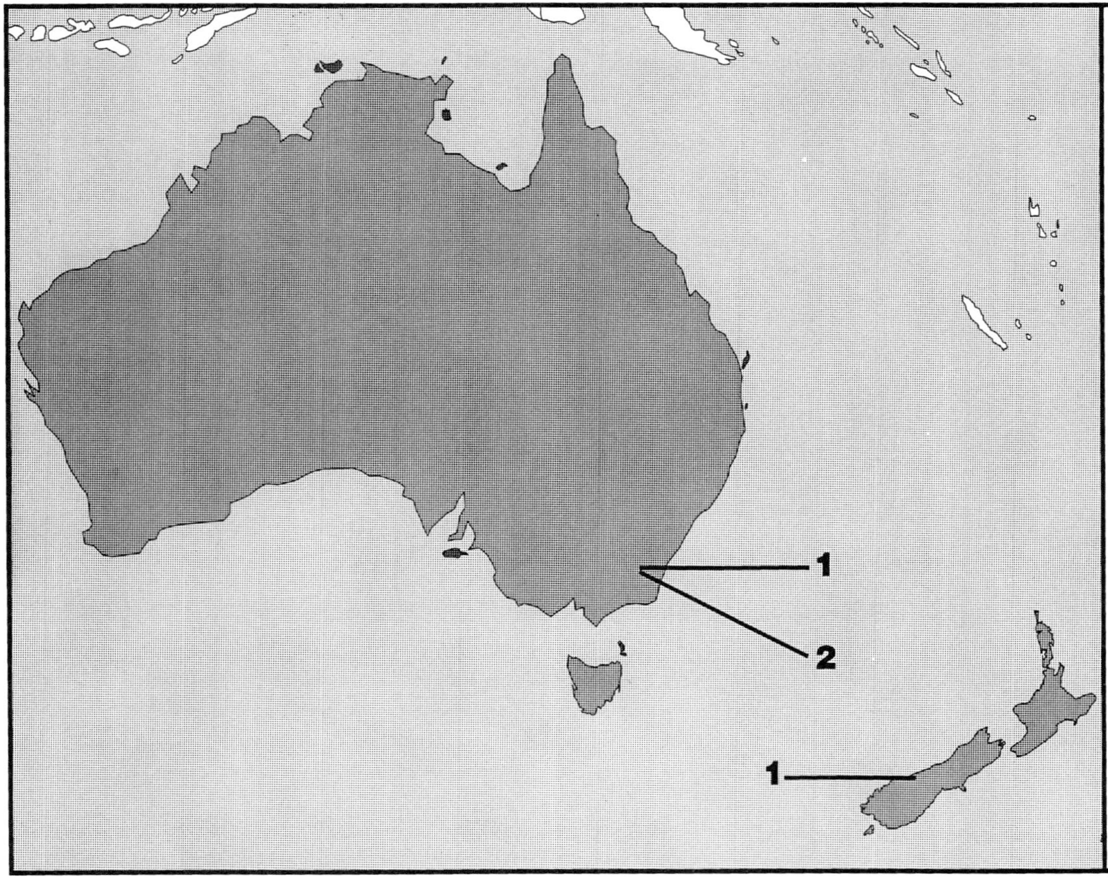

Operation Starlight - Australia and New Zealand

Australia

1 Mount Kosciusko

2 Mount Ramshead

New Zealand

1 Mount Wakefield

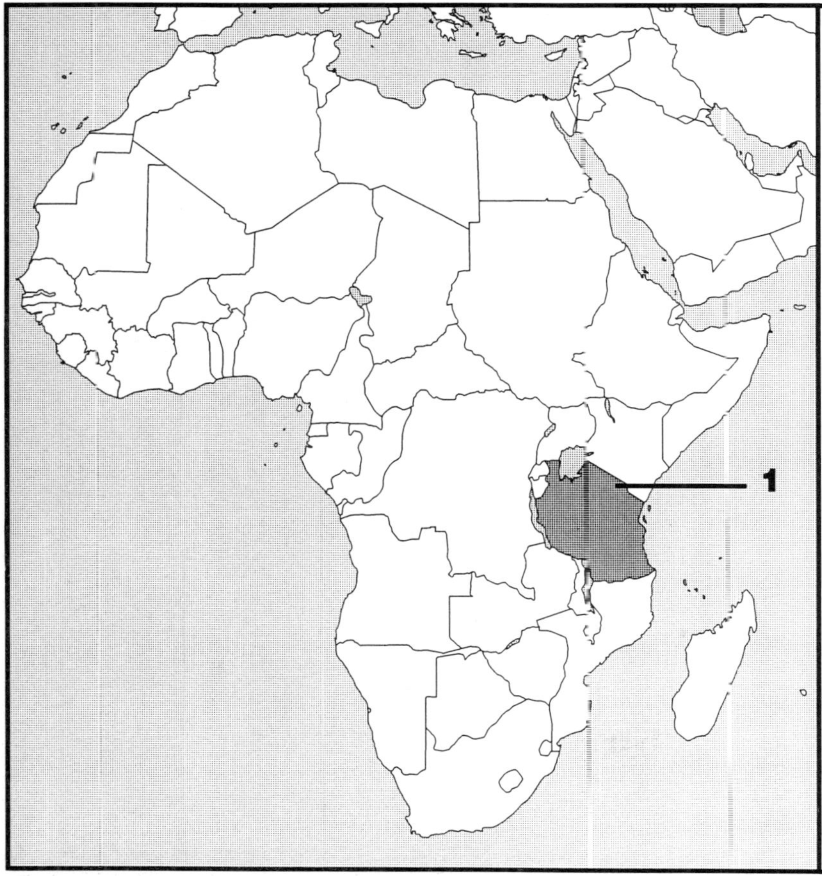

Operation Starlight in Tanzania, Africa

1 Mount Kilimanjaro

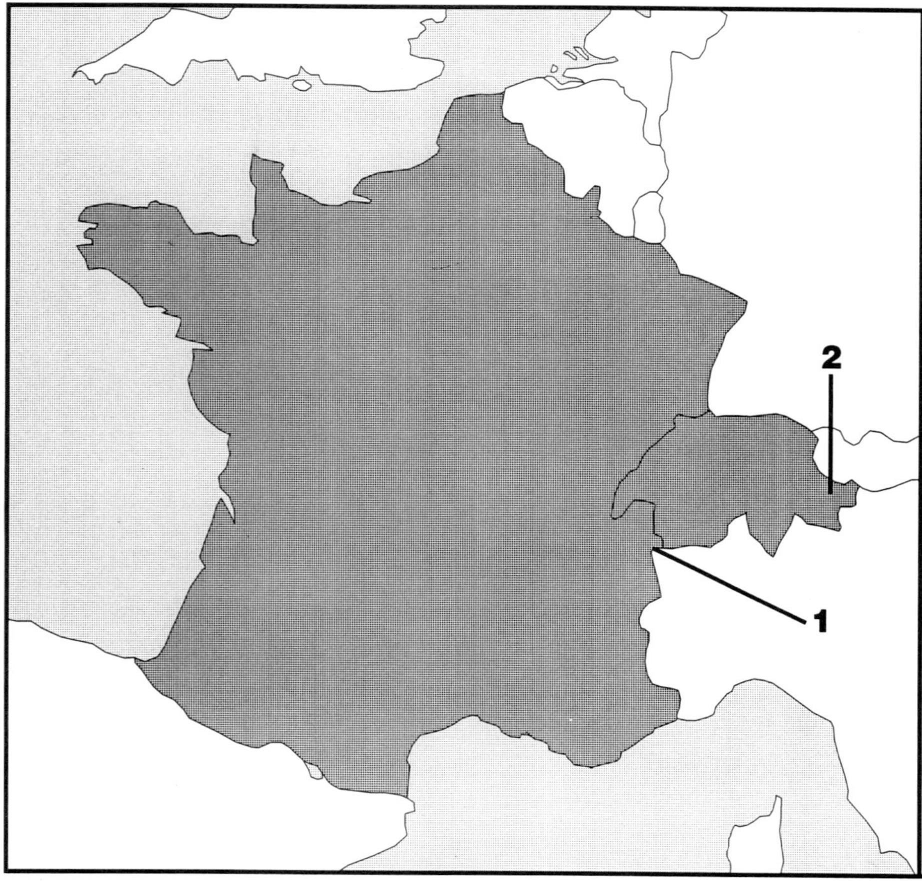

Operation Starlight in France and Switzerland

France

1 Le Nid D'Aigle

Switzerland

2 Mount Madrigerfluh

CHAPTER 3

THE LORD'S DECLARATION

"There will shortly come Another among you. (1)

"He will stand tall among men with a shining countenance. This One will be attired in a single garment of the type now known to you. His shoes will be soft-topped, yet not made of the skin of animals. (2)

"He will approach the Earth Leaders. They will ask of Him His credentials. He will produce these. (3)

"His magic will be greater than any upon the Earth – greater than the combined materialistic might of all the armies. And they who heed not His Words shall be removed from the Earth. (4)

"This Rock is now Holy and will remain so for as long as the World exists.

"Go ye forth and spread My Word throughout the World, so that all men of pure heart **may prepare for His coming."**

Question;

"How shall I prove to men that this Rock is Charged with Your Power?"

Answer:

"Bid the unbelievers to stand thereon and when the Sun returneth to the exact position as that you see now, they will know that this is so! (5)

"Therefore, put ye a mark upon the rock that the angle may be know to all. And let the Pilgrims stand thus. (6)

"But say ye this – **Whosoever, knowing these things, defaces this MY ROCK, shall destroy himself.**

"Go ye forth as Commanded and speak of this to all...!"

A Lord of Karma on Brown Willy
Sunday, November 23rd, 1958. 2:30 p.m. - 2:45 p.m.

NOTES ON "THE LORD'S DECLARATION"

This powerful Declaration was made to our Master, His Eminence Sir George King, Primary Terrestrial Mental Channel for Interplanetary Parliament, by a **LORD OF KARMA,** immediately after he had served as terrestrial anchor for the Charging of Brown Willy in Cornwall, England, during Phase Two of Operation Starlight in the British Isles. Brown Willy was Charged as a Holy Mountain of the world by a LORD OF KARMA.

NOTE 1. The term, "Another," is a reference to the Next Master, or next World Avatar, Who will appear upon Earth **when the time is right!** He will appear at a critical time, when conditions upon Earth are prepared for His Coming, as determined by The Lords Of Karma. This Great One will not be the Master Jesus, but, like Jesus, a Mighty Interplanetary Being! Readers are referred to "Interplanetary Existence" in our Master's book, *The Nine Freedoms.*

NOTE 2. Our Master wrote: "When this was said, I felt as though a one-piece suit of elastic-like material enclosed my body from neck to ankles in a pleasant, warm, resilient but firm grip. I felt a strange lightness at this time."

The garment worn by the Next Master will be produced by Him by His mental processes, specifically for the requirements of His appearance upon Earth. As such, it will be instantly changeable by Him as conditions merit.

NOTE 3. This Mighty Being will not be limited as past Avatars have been, in that He will be allowed by The Karmic Lords to demonstrate His Divine Powers as needed. His "credentials" might be, for instance, the floating of the Statue of Liberty high above New York City.

NOTE 4. Whatever demonstration is made or whatever is spoken by this Mighty One, there will be those upon Earth who will call Him anti-Christ, enemy of the people, or a threat to "national security." No opposition of any kind will prevail, however. The Next Master will usher in the New Age of World Peace and Enlightenment for all who are ready, as The Logos Of Earth enters Her New Age! "They who heed not His words" will literally be "removed from the Earth" to be reborn upon another, younger World — now in existence within the Solar System — there to "relive the terrors of the history they have made upon this Planet!" Readers are referred to "The Next Master Is Coming" and "The Bright New Dawn" in our Master's book, *The Day The Gods Came.*

NOTE 5. This statement refers to the exact position of the Sun in relation to our Master's position at that instant, i.e. between 2:30 p.m. and 2:45 p.m. G.M.T. on November 23rd, 1958, or equivalent. The exact position of the Sun — at a given time and day — will only vary a few fractions of a second in altitude and azimuth from year to year. To all practical intents and purposes, the "exact position" of the Sun does not require additional calculation.

NOTE 6. "And let the pilgrims stand thus," is a very significant statement inasmuch as the Great One referred to the benefits of a pilgrimage to this particular spot. Hundreds of such pilgrimages have been made to date and many wonderful experiences have been reported.

It was later revealed by our Master that Brown Willy was unique in being dual-poled, with separate positively and negatively Charged Rocks at the Charged Spot. The negatively Charged Rock was marked by painting with a cross, which pilgrims may face from the positively Charged Rock.

"THE LORD'S DECLARATION" was first published in *Cosmic Voice,* Issue No. 19, March-April 1959, and is now out of print. It continues to be essential that this great Truth be made known throughout all the Earth!

CHAPTER 4

THE COSMIC MASTERS SPEAK!

The great Cosmic Masters delivered many Messages regarding Operation Starlight through our Master. Some of these Messages were delivered to him mentally on a Holy Mountain just following the Charge, and contained vital information specific to the Mountain and its Charge. These are presented below for the reader's study. Others were delivered through our Master at other times, while he was in a positive, self-induced Yogic Samadhic trance. These Messages were more general in nature and pertained to Operation Starlight as a whole. Selected Messages of this type are also presented here for your study.

On Brown Willy, Cornwall, England; November 23rd, 1958:

"The Lord's Declaration," given to our Master mentally at this time, is reprinted in Chapter 3.

About Mount Baldy, Southern California, U.S.A.; August 9th, 1959:

"The Power in the first mountain Charged as a Cosmic Age Power Centre in the Americas has properties peculiar to its Cosmic position. By that, I mean the Energies which can be contacted by the performance of 'The Twelve Blessings' upon Mount Baldy are those Energies which should be used for general radiation purposes, **so that all the life streams upon Terra who are ready for these particular Energies may avail themselves of the Energies as the teams of pilgrims radiate them.**

"The Energies of Mount Baldy help the pilgrims to have a deeper Cosmic appreciation."

THE MASTER AETHERIUS

On Mount Tallac, Northern California, U.S.A.; October 21st, 1959:

"This place is now Holy for it is Charged with **MY POWER.** And when, through change, this mountain falleth, every rock shall be as a living jewel radiating **MY LOVE** to they who, with pure heart do serve the Great Cause, that of bringing into being the unification of all mankind in Spiritual Enlightenment.

"Take up thy staff and go forth and speak of this. Bid the pilgrims to come hither, so that they may radiate to all, the Light now in this glistening jewel in the Body of She Whose sacrifice gave unto man the opportunity to realize his Divinity."

THE MASTER JESUS

About Mount Tallac; October 22nd, 1959:

"The Energies now potential within the second mountain (in the Americas) help the pilgrims to **realize the vital part which they play in the preparation of Terra for a Spiritual Renaissance.**"

THE MASTER AETHERIUS

On Mount Adams, New Hampshire, U.S.A.; March 15th, 1960:

"This mountain is now Charged with Energies which, when activated correctly, will manifest in that balance necessary to heal those terrestrials whose Karmic pattern allows such intervention.

"If you would serve your brothers, come ye to the summit, activate this potential and radiate these Energies to all who need such help."

MARS SECTOR 6

About Castle Peak, Colorado, U.S.A.; May 14th, 1960:

"I would like to extend a Commendation from all Members of The Great White Brotherhood to those gallant Few who successfully completed Operation Starlight in the Americas. There are no words to fully express Our appreciation to these choice Few, who, by dint of their courage, made possible this magnificent task; made possible a move which enabled certain of Us to come nearer to so-called civilization."

THE MASTER SAINT GOO-LING

On Mount Kosciusko, New South Wales, Australia; December 5th, 1960:

"There will come a day when all who are then in this country will come in pilgrimage to this place. A realization of the significance of the Power herein will gradually dawn upon them and they will radiate this Energy to the whole of Terra.

"This act will be as an initiation into the realms of selfless expansion which can only spring from the womb of Service.

"Mark this well, man — there will not be a single part of your land which will assume a greater importance for you than this spot.

"It is done. Go you forth and tell the Australians that the Power within each atom here is more valuable to them than all they possess — and more lasting. . . !"

THE MASTER AETHERIUS

On Mount Ramshead, New South Wales, Australia; December 8th, 1960:

"This Rock is now Charged with potential Energies which have certain basic characteristics. The potential, when activated by Spiritual practise on this spot, can be radiated to those who are mentally and physically sick. The workers who perform such a terrestrial service will themselves be magnetized to such an extent as to enable them to render healing to some who need this.

"There is much sickness upon Terra. Many need help. Use these Energies and help them.

"This action was taken with the Sanction and Authority of Interplanetary Parliament based upon the Planet — Saturn.

"Come — Pray — Heal."

MARS SECTOR 6

On Mount Wakefield, South Island, New Zealand; December 24th, 1960:

"Oh My son, you have done well.

"The land can now rejoice for this place is Consecrated with My Blessing. I say now that the Power herein can be sent into the hearts of all men.

"As fire cannot exist without fuel, neither can the Flame of Love within the heart of man live without expression. True expression is Service and Service is donation through unselfish effort.

"Bid the pilgrims to come hither and send this, My Power, unto mankind through Prayer, so that he may become wise enough to allow his highest attribute, that of Love's expression, to manifest as unselfish Service."

THE MASTER JESUS

About Operation Starlight to that time; July 17th, 1961:

"Operation Starlight is the most important single Occult task ever undertaken on this Earth for the last 100,000 years."

THE MASTER SAINT GOO-LING

About Operation Starlight after its completion; July 27th, 1962:

"OPERATION STARLIGHT IS THE GREATEST SINGLE META-PHYSICAL TASK EVER UNDERTAKEN UPON TERRA IN THIS HER PRESENT LIFE."

THE MASTER AETHERIUS

Other Cosmic Messages:

Thousands of words were spoken by The Cosmic Masters about Operation Starlight and it is not possible to reprint this vast store of information in this book. There were, however, some vital points made which are briefly recounted below:

1. After Operation Starlight was completed, all the Holy Mountains were interlinked by the Masters in such a way

that pilgrims activating the Energies on one Holy Mountain through themselves, activated the Energies in all.

2. The special Energies in Ben Hope, Castle Peak and Mount Kilimanjaro would not be interchanged with the other Holy Mountains "as yet."
3. Operation Starlight had made it possible for The Spiritual Hierarchy Of Earth to move from relative isolation closer to mankind by establishing new Retreats in Ben MacDhui and Castle Peak.

OVER 600 COSMIC TRANSMISSIONS

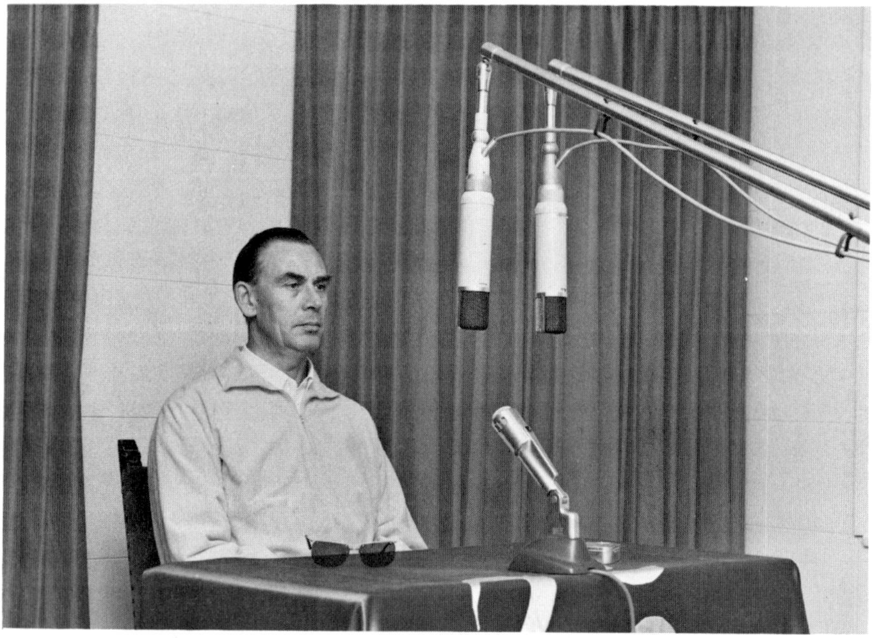

His Eminence Sir George King has received and recorded over 600 Cosmic Transmissions while in positive, Yogic Samadhic trance. These have been copied for archival storage in secure vaults for posterity.

NEW RETREAT IN COLORADO

Castle Peak, Colorado. Our Master and his Team rest on the snowy slopes below the towering summit of Castle Peak in the Rocky Mountains of Colorado. One of the outstanding repercussions of Operation Starlight was that The Spiritual Hierarchy Of Earth, the Ascended Masters of The Great White Brotherhood, were able to move closer to so-called civilization by occupying some of the Charged Mountains as Retreats. Such Retreats are actually Temples and workplaces located within or under the mountains, where the Ascended Masters carry out their work of 'holding the Light' on Earth. These Masters now occupy Castle Peak, bringing closer that day in the New Age when They will begin to walk openly among mankind, dispensing Their vast Wisdom to all.

NEW RETREAT IN SCOTLAND

Ben MacDhui and Craig-An-Leth-Chain, Scotland. Seen from across Loch Morlich, the Cairngorms Range contains both Craig-An-Leth-Chain, Charged through our Master on December 14th, 1958, by a Lord Of Karma; and Ben MacDhui, the major peak in the range, which became a new Retreat for The Spiritual Hierarchy Of Earth afterward. This was another example of the Ascended Masters moving closer to mankind due to Operation Starlight.

ANCIENT RETREAT IN AFRICA

Mount Kilimanjaro, Tanzania. This majestic mountain, the highest in the African continent, has long been an important Retreat for The Spiritual Hierarchy. Following its Charging in July 1961 in Operation Starlight, it has assumed an even greater importance than before. Distance is deceptive, for the main peak of Mount Kilimanjaro rises 3½ miles above the flatlands in the foreground of this photograph. Uhuru Peak is five days away!

CHAPTER 5

OPERATION STARLIGHT PLUS

His Eminence Sir George King performed Operation Starlight between July 23rd, 1958, and August 23rd, 1961 — a period of 37 months which, with minimal financial means at his disposal, saw him travelling throughout most of the Western Hemisphere; from the northern tip of Scotland to the sub-Equatorial antipodes, as well as from Europe to the United States. The Charging alone of 18 Holy Mountains during this period would have been an exhausting physical feat. His Eminence's task was not limited to physical exertion, however, but included the spreading of the Teachings of The Cosmic Masters which he had already received, as well as receiving and disseminating new Teachings from these Elevated Sources as the Mission progressed! A brief outline of this superhuman and entirely successful effort is presented below.

76 COSMIC TRANSMISSIONS

These include:

The Twelve Blessings
The Nine Freedoms
The Next Master Is Coming
Tread Carefully Ye Men
Appeal To World Citizens
What Is Death?
The Council's Decision
The Importance Of Power Absorption
Three Adepts On Earth
The Cosmic Plan
Rise, Oh Man
Cooperation Will Save You
Fight Ye The Evil
Prepare Ye, Oh Men
The Initiation Of Earth
The New World
Message To America
Be Not Limited

231 LECTURES, PRESS, RADIO AND TELEVISION INTERVIEWS

In large convention halls or small public meetings; in airport passenger lounges or in media studios, our Master made himself available in three continents and in 12 American States, to present the true Teachings of The Cosmic Masters, with the clear and simple explanation of these which flowed from his own profound and enlightened understanding.

NEARLY 65,000 MILES!

Travelling by ocean freighter, propellor-driven aircraft, aging personal or rental automobiles, or on foot, our Master covered an incredible distance during Operation Starlight! The late 1950's were without the jet aircraft and modern freeways or other conveniences which we take for granted today! Motel and hotel accommodations then bore little resemblance to those of our age. Mountain gear of the period was massive, heavyweight and primitive when compared with what is now available in almost any sporting goods shop! Nevertheless our Master made a series of journeys accumulating nearly 65,000 miles by conservative estimate, in order to fulfill the instructions given him by The Cosmic Masters to spread Their Teachings and this Mission throughout the world!

Here, indeed, is a modern three-year odyssey beyond compare — especially considering the hardships suffered, and the benefits to mankind which we are, even now, only beginning to realize!

SPREADING THE TEACHINGS

Our Master on the Tom Duggan TV show in July 1960, just before demonstrating a Samadhic trance state during which The Master Aetherius gave a brief Transmission over a national network station before a respectfully hushed anchor and camera crew, with specially dimmed lighting.

Only one of many lectures and conventions attended by our Master during Operation Starlight to spread the Teachings, this one in Gibson Hall in Los Angeles featured colour slides of the Charging of Castle Peak, which had just been completed a few months earlier.

CHAPTER 6

OPERATION STARLIGHT — A COSMIC SEED

Operation Starlight — a brilliant and far-reaching Cosmic Mission itself, has also led to several other extremely important Missions, both directly and indirectly.

One of the most important repercussions from Operation Starlight is the brilliant Karmic Mission OPERATION SUNBEAM. His Eminence combined Operation Starlight with knowledge gained from other Missions of The Aetherius Society, and created OPERATION SUNBEAM, a Mission designed to help the Mother Earth directly.

His Eminence knows through personal experience that the Mother Earth is a highly evolved and compassionate Goddess Herself. She has given mankind a home for millions of years, protecting and nurturing us, despite the coarse and vile way we have treated Her through our wars, our pollution and other acts against Her nature.

The vast majority of mankind do not even know She is a living, breathing Entity!

OPERATION SUNBEAM

His Eminence, knowing the great debt we all owe the Mother Earth, was deeply inspired to create a Mission whereby mankind could begin to give back to Her at least a token amount of Spiritual Energy. In OPERATION SUNBEAM, the Energy is invoked from the 19 Holy Mountains Charged in Operation Starlight. A portion of this Holy Spiritual Energy meant for mankind is collected and given instead, in sacrifice, to the Mother Earth through certain Psychic Centres within Her body. We have been told most definitely by The Cosmic

Masters Themselves that OPERATION SUNBEAM and its brilliant Karmic manipulation has benefited mankind tremendously since its inception. Without Operation Starlight, OPERATION SUNBEAM would not exist today as we know it.

This magnificent Spiritual Mission is still being performed today by The Aetherius Society and will continue into the future. We strongly urge anyone reading this book who has not heard of this essential Mission to learn more about it in our other publications. (Note 1.)

THE GREAT WHITE BROTHERHOOD

Another important and very interesting change stemming from Operation Starlight was the movement of two major Retreats, or Branches, of The Spiritual Hierarchy Of Earth into two of the Holy Mountains: Castle Peak in Colorado, U.S.A., and Ben MacDhui in Scotland. This small, elite group of Ascended Masters, known as The Great White Brotherhood, have only been allowed limited contact with mankind in the past due to mankind's Karmic limitations. However, as the New Age draws nearer and the numbers of Spiritual workers increase, contact between The Great White Brotherhood and mankind will slowly expand. This significant move out from the remote Himalayas to areas closer to humanity is a major step in that direction — a step greatly facilitated by Operation Starlight. (Note 2.)

"THE TWELVE BLESSINGS"

"The Twelve Blessings," a series of twelve Transmissions of advanced Teachings from the Master Jesus, was also closely connected to Operation Starlight. These Holy Transmissions commenced on July 27th, 1958, just four days after this same elevated Cosmic Master Charged Holdstone Down through His Eminence, marking the start of Operation Starlight. This New Age Bible is an extension of His Sermon on the Mount and adds a Cosmic Concept to religious study and practice hitherto unknown by man on Earth.

It has been said by The Cosmic Masters that the mystical practice of "The Twelve Blessings" upon one of the Charged Mountains during a Spiritual Push is the most potent Spiritual practice common man is able to perform in these days. (Note 3.)

OPERATION PRAYER POWER

The Aetherius Society uses "The Twelve Blessings" ritual in many ways, one of which is in OPERATION PRAYER POWER, another Cosmic Mission now being performed by The Aetherius Society, with roots indirectly in Operation Starlight. In OPERATION PRAYER POWER His Eminence has designed radionic equipment whereby Spiritual Energy invoked through trained Prayer Teams performing "The Twelve Blessings" can be stored in a Spiritual Energy Battery and be built up over the course of several months or even years. This potent Energy can then be released in a highly concentrated Energy stream whenever it is most needed by the world; for example, for the relief of earthquake victims, or even to help prevent a war.

The radionic equipment used in OPERATION PRAYER POWER was based upon the equipment designed and built for OPERATION SUNBEAM. Both the equipment and "The Twelve Blessings" ritual had their start in Operation Starlight.

OPERATION PRAYER POWER is an on-going Mission of The Aetherius Society and one in which all are invited to help. (Note 4.)

OPERATION POWER LIGHT

The most recent development in The Aetherius Society has been the inauguration of a new Spiritual Mission called OPERATION POWER LIGHT. In this Cosmic Mission, Spiritual Energy is manipulated through our Master, His Eminence Sir George King, and at times other Agencies, to promote World Healing and Upliftment. The Cosmic Master responsible for inventing this Mission and for manipulating the Energy, is

Mars Sector 8—Special Advisor S2, Whom we believe to be closely associated with the Great Master Mars Sector 8, one of the Cosmic Beings Who Charged the Holy Mountain Ben Hope. (Note 5.)

During Phase 12 of OPERATION POWER LIGHT, for the first time in this Mission, the source of Spiritual Energy manipulated through His Eminence and other Agencies was from a Holy Mountain. Interestingly enough, the first mountain used was Ben Hope! We are quite certain that as this Mission progresses, there will be formed an even closer bond with the Holy Mountains of the world, giving these wonderful Spiritual Batteries yet another potent outlet for their life-giving Energies.

The above is a partial account of just a few of the outstanding Spiritual fruits growing from the Cosmic Seed — Operation Starlight. As can clearly be seen, the world would indeed be a much darker place were it not for Operation Starlight and its effects. We can only conjecture what tremendous happenings will be inspired in the future from these gifts from The Gods — the glorious 19 Holy Mountains of the world!

NOTE 1. Further understanding of OPERATION SUNBEAM can be gained by a study of the following Aetherius Society publications: Cassette No. C-54, *Operation Sunbeam;* Metacassette® No. MC-2, *Operation Sunbeam Inspires The Galaxy;* and Metacassette® No. MC-19, *Gotha Speaks To Earth.* Also read, *Operation Sunbeam — God's Magic In Action;* and *Eternal Recognition Of Operation Sunbeam.*

The history of this Mission has also been recorded in The Aetherius Society Newsletter and the Journal *Cosmic Voice.* Details are available from the publishers, The Aetherius Society.

NOTE 2. For information about The Spiritual Hierarchy Of Earth, study Cassette No. C-23, *The Great White Brotherhood — The Spiritual Hierarchy Of Ascended Mas-*

ters; also the booklets: *My Contact With The Great White Brotherhood; A Special Assignment;* and *The Festival Of 'Carrying The Light'.*

NOTE 3. The beautiful "Twelve Blessings" Transmissions are available in book form, as well as on Metacassette® Album No. MC-27. An in-depth explanation by His Eminence of these Transmissions is also available on Cassette Album No. C-73, *The Lectures On The Twelve Blessings.*

NOTE 4. To learn more about OPERATION PRAYER POWER, study of the following Aetherius Society publications is recommended: Cassette No. C-52, *Operation Prayer Power;* Metacassette® No. MC-12, *Operation Prayer Power — A Spiritual Dream Come True;* Metacassette® No. MC-13, *Important Declaration Of Truth To Terra;* and Metacassette® No. MC-21, *The Inauguration Of Operation Prayer Power On Level Four.*

The history of this Mission has also been recorded in *The Aetherius Society Newsletter* and the Journal *Cosmic Voice.* Details are obtainable from the publishers, The Aetherius Society.

For information on how to participate in this ongoing Mission, contact your nearest Headquarters or Branch of The Aetherius Society and read the pamphlet *Operation Prayer Power — A Spiritual Dream Come True,* obtainable free of charge.

NOTE 5. Information on the early Phases of OPERATION POWER LIGHT is published in *Cosmic Voice,* Volume 14, Issues 5-8; Issues 16-17; and Issues 18-21, 1993.

OPERATION PRAYER POWER ON HOLDSTONE DOWN

The Mission **Operation Prayer Power** was inaugurated on Holdstone Down on June 30th, 1973. Spiritual Energies invoked through recitation of Holy Mantra are directed towards a Team skilled in the science of dynamic Prayer, who convey the Energies into a specially-designed Battery capable of holding thousands of hours of this Prayer Energy for long periods of time. This stored Energy can later be released through a Spiritual Energy Radiator to any part of the world to relieve suffering caused by disasters, such as earthquakes, famine or war.

CHAPTER 7

GROUP EXPERIENCES ON HOLY MOUNTAINS

The world is full of sceptics, doubters and sneerers. It is in total disregard of such unfortunates that we present in this Chapter a few selected sacred experiences shared by a group of people on some of the Holy Mountains of the world Charged during Operation Starlight. There are hundreds of private, personal experiences reported which were not shared by other persons. Recognizing that this in no way invalidates or lessens the private experience, we have elected to present only those which were shared by several individuals simultaneously.

The Holy Being on Mount Baldy

In late October of 1961, Charles Abrahamson and Irene Noppe hoped, with five other ladies, to make the final pilgrimage of the season to Mount Baldy. The weather was already extremely cold, with a freezing wind.

Crossing the "Devil's Backbone," about 100 yards ahead of the rest of the party, Charles psychically saw a Scout Patrol-type Spacecraft leaving the Charged Rock which, from that point, was still out of sight. This Spacecraft was translucent, as though carved from ice and back-lighted. This incident was entirely private and is only described here because of what followed.

About 45 minutes later, still in advance of the strung-out party, Charles came into view of the Charged Spot, about 300 yards ahead. At that moment, he was literally frozen in his tracks by a powerful sensation in his Heart Centre, together with an audible, deep cyclic VRUM-VRUM-VRUM sound emanating from the Charged Rock ahead.

Looking up from the loose scree at the Charged Rock, Charles saw another translucent figure — this time a shrouded, bare-headed male about nine to ten feet in height — standing by the Charged Spot and looking away toward the east. At no time during any of what follows did He acknowledge the pilgrims' presence or even appear to notice them!

Seconds later, Irene Noppe stepped past Charles and froze — putting her right hand to her heart — and turned to stare at Charles in amazement. Charles signalled Irene to give no indication to the others who, one by one, passed the leaders and — one by one — froze in mid-step. Only one young lady, not an Aetherius Society Member and with no experience of exercise of any kind, did not share this experience. She was insensitive from sheer exhaustion.

The group of six quietly compared notes, finding that their experiences were identical. Inasmuch as they had already begun a ritual in climbing the Holy Mountain, they decided to go ahead with their intended Prayer Circle at the Charged Spot! They approached the Being, formed a semi-circle near Him, and began the Service of The Twelve Blessings. He remained until somewhere near the Tenth or Eleventh Blessing, and then He vanished. Often during the Service, all six from time to time understandably took a quick look. There He was, only a few yards from them — tall, powerful, utterly silent and unmoving — until suddenly, He was gone!

Mount Tallac Effort Rewarded

Earlier in 1961, Charles and Irene drove all night from Los Angeles for a pilgrimage to Mount Tallac during the July 4th holiday long weekend. Northern California had been in the grip of a severe drought for over six months. Not a drop of rain had fallen and none was forecast. On their arrival at Fallen Leaf Lake at 7:00 a.m., the temperature was already nearly 90° F. Parking near the last private cabin from where they intended to start their climb, they told the middle-aged couple who lived there during the summer of their intentions to climb Mount

Tallac and to camp overnight at Pyramid Lake en route.

By noon, they had barely made it halfway to the lake. The heat was over 100°, without a cloud in the sky. With their heavy packs of food, tents and sleeping gear, they thought of turning back. Instead, they opted to rest in place and wait for the Sun to begin to set. About four hours later, they successfully reached Pyramid Lake and made camp, climbing to the Charged Rock the next morning for several Services before returning to the lake.

The rain began to fall at 8:00 p.m., built to a downpour through the night, and only ceased about 8:00 a.m. as the pilgrims broke camp!

At the cabin below, the occupants fed them a huge and delicious breakfast and **demanded** to know what they had been doing on Mount Tallac! They seemed completely unsurprised at the full and honest reply, announcing without hesitation and with utter determination, that the pilgrims' Prayers had broken the drought!

UFO's Over Holdstone Down

Throughout the years there have been many reports of Unidentified Flying Objects by pilgrims on the Holy Mountains of the world. We briefly describe below one of the best.

On May 14th, 1977, a Special Power Circle was held on Holdstone Down where over 100 pilgrims were led in Prayer by our Master, the Power released from the mountain being dedicated to healing the sick throughout the world.

The Power Circle lasted some two hours, after which the pilgrims departed, except for the OPERATION SUNBEAM Team who were to stay overnight on the mountain. The Power was kept flowing for several more hours by Dynamic Prayer Teams until OPERATION SUNBEAM began, and great Spiritual Energies from Holdstone Down were relayed by Cosmic Intelligences to be directed to The Logos Of Earth.

Shortly thereafter — from 10:00 p.m. until 1:30 a.m. — the skies above Holdstone Down became alive with several dozen

Flying Saucers! There were 11 members of the Team on the mountain that night, including our Master and his wife Monique, together with Alan Moseley, Ray Nielsen, Jimmy Gourlay, David Barton, Bernard Stinchcombe, Michael Barnes, Beryl Lawton, Peter Simmons and John Holder.

At least five UFO's were seen at one time by the entire Team, including one sighting where the Object stopped in the sky, performed a corkscrew flight pattern and disappeared! Many of the other Objects performed flight patterns which could not be duplicated by any man-made aircraft, such as zig-zag reciprocal patterns, 90 degree turns, stopping in mid-flight, disappearing and reappearing again, triangular manoeuvres and the like. These were not so-called natural phenomena, but could only have been manufactured objects under intelligent control!

What had begun as a very calm, cloudless night became a Flying Saucer spotter's dream. Several of the Team had more than one sighting at the same time and it literally became difficult to keep count of them all! Such, obviously, was the interest shown by Extra-Terrestrial Visitors in the really important happenings on our world!

Fuller details of this amazing experience are contained on The Aetherius Society Cassette No. 53, *The Occult Significance of Flying Saucers,* a lecture by our Master.

Proof Given On Brown Willy

On November 23rd, 1981, the 23rd anniversary of the Charging of Brown Willy, The Aetherius Society Torquay Group Organizer led a pilgrimage to this mysterious Holy Mountain to ascertain how the statement made 23 years earlier by a Lord Of Karma might be manifested.

Brenda Ward, with her son Philip Taylor and her daughter-in-law Kate, went to Brown Willy with a friend, Maureen Claye, who technically qualified as a "non-believer." Their intention was to stand as directed by the Lord Of Karma as the Sun returned to the exact position it had been in when the mountain was Charged through our Master.

Although the weather was cold and overcast — and grew worse as they journeyed through Cornwall — they hoped for an improvement long enough for them to make the climb. By the time they had reached Rough Tor it was pouring with rain and, due to the danger of the surrounding moors, they almost decided to return home. Deciding to wait instead, they were rewarded by a sudden ceasing of the downpour. Quickly donning their wet-weather gear, they made the climb in the cold wind under a sky heavy with black clouds. At the summit, they performed a Twelve Blessings Service and then found what little shelter they could among the rocks to wait for the exact time to arrive.

Philip had an accurate watch which he had set correctly and, at precisely 2:30 p.m., they were back on the positive Charged Rock to begin their Service again. Only Philip could stand in the fierce winds, so the three women knelt on the Rock instead. They faced the negative Rock where a cross had been painted and continued their Prayers.

Suddenly, in front and to the left of them, the dense black clouds opened and an intense beam of brilliant sunlight illuminated them like a spotlight amid the darkness of the surrounding moor!

They were, naturally, dumbstruck with awe for a moment, until the friend, Maureen, burst into tears saying, "I've never known anything like it!"

Then, as suddenly as it had come, the sunlight was gone and the moor returned to its cold, forbidding appearance.

The pilgrims had not expected a physical manifestation, but rather some sort of inner conviction to come upon them. In fact, they all agreed they had experienced **BOTH**, and the sense of inner conviction only grew as they recollected the experience later! Indeed, the Lord's statement made in 1958 had, for them, been literally fulfilled!

(See "The Lord's Declaration" in Chapter 3.)

White-Robed Figures on Mount Adams

In July 1987, Elaine Gay and Jane Holubik from the Toronto

Group, with John Welch of the Michigan Branch, climbed Mount Adams with a larger group of Members and held a Service at the Charged Rock. The group stayed overnight at the Madison Hut and intended to return for a second Service the following day.

Elaine, Jane and John, feeling unwell, elected to hold their Service lower down at Star Lake.

During a break between Prayers, they heard a Twelve Blessings Service in progress on the peak, about 1,000 feet higher in elevation! They looked up at the location where the Service was being held to see several people dressed in white. They were surprised to see white clothing because they could not recall any one of their party wearing white when they set out for the climb. When the larger group returned from the peak, they indeed were not wearing white, nor did they have any white clothing in their packs.

The consensus was that the lower group had either seen white light shining from the praying individuals, or that they saw other Beings Who had joined in with the Service on the Charged Spot.

Our Master On Mount Baldy

Large pilgrimages of from 50 to 100 people were made throughout 1960 and 1961 to Mount Baldy, and it became commonplace for employees at the lodge 2,000 feet below to report brilliant beams of White Light flashing into the sky during these pilgrimages.

In the summer of 1962, His Eminence decided that we should film, in 16mm Kodachrome, a re-creation of the Charging of the mountain, which had been filmed in amateur 8mm.

The original Team, wearing the identical clothing, began the climb, with Charles Abrahamson — not a member of the Charging Team — filming with a Bell & Howell Filmo turret camera.

Just below the Charged Rock, Monique and Irene Noppe, with Keith Robertson, halted as they had done two years earlier, while our Master went ahead to perform the Charge alone. Charles was mid-way between them and, with a long pan of the camera, filmed our Master climbing up, past him, and away to the Charged Spot which was visible in the camera view-finder.

When the film was processed, a very interesting thing was noticed as the **original** footage was examined. His Eminence, approaching the Charged Spot, walked directly **through** a multi-coloured, almost transparent object exactly in the shape and size of the "skirt" of a Scout Patrol Spacecraft.

Rushing back to Consolidated Film Laboratories (CFI) in Hollywood, where the film had been processed, our Master had the original footage examined by their chief of quality control. This expert checked the frame lines, the first and last frames showing the strange object, and found no evidence that the film had been light-struck in camera, or fogged during development — either of which would have overlapped the frame lines! His firm, unshakeable technical analysis? Whatever the object was, it had been photographed through the lens. Pressed further, he replied simply, "Psychic phenomena!"

This footage will be included in an upcoming video production of the Charging of Mount Baldy. What a group experience **that** will be!

CHAPTER 8

GUIDE FOR PILGRIMS

The Holy Mountains of the world Charged in Operation Starlight, while offering unprecedented Spiritual opportunities to pilgrims, also present a number of very practical considerations which must be taken into account. The Karmic Lord Mars Sector 6 Himself said, *"What is SERVICE but Love in practical action."*

Without discounting Service or Love, we wish here to underscore **practical** action. Pilgrims must avoid all unnecessary risk of accident, injury or illness which might result from a pilgrimage undertaken without due regard for age, health, physical condition; improper or inadequate clothing or equipment; insufficient food and water; or ignorance of or disregard for climatic and terrain conditions.

The Aetherius Society has prepared this Guide to help pilgrims to plan for most conditions and eventualities on the Holy Mountains.

The British Isles

Holdstone Down: One of the most frequented Holy Mountains, suitable for people of all ages and accessible throughout the entire year. The elevation is 1,140 feet. The Charged Spot is a 20-minute walk from Hunter's Inn road, outside the village of Combe Martin. Pilgrims should check weather forecasts and be prepared for high winds and heavy rain at times.

Brown Willy: At 1,377 feet in the middle of England's mysterious and treacherous Bodmin Moor, a pilgrimage here definitely should not be made alone on the first occasion. The route to this mountain is a strict one, as dangerous marshes present a hazard. During the Second World War, during training manoeuvres, an American heavy tank disappeared without a trace, sinking into the deep marshes! Approximately a 90-minute walk from the nearest main road, this mountain does not present much of a climb except for the last 20 minutes. Recommended approach is from Camelford, via Rough Tor. Climbable most of the year, but should be avoided during periods of heavy rain, when the marshes are deep and dangerous; or in fog, when a hiker can become easily lost.

(For text of the Mental Contact on Brown Willy, see: "The Lord's Declaration" in Chapter 3.)

Ben Hope: This is the most remotely situated Holy Mountain in the British Isles, some 30 miles from the nearest habitation in the village of Tongue. Prospective climbers should first report to the Tongue Estate Office, since deer-stalking parties are often arranged to the mountain, and shooting takes place. At 3,040 feet, the Charged Rock is situated at the very summit and presents a long, arduous climb of two to three hours under the best of conditions. Very exposed to the elements. Only attempt this climb in the summer months when sufficient daylight is available. Correct climbing equipment is absolutely essential. Best approach is from the south, starting near the waterfall.

Craig-An-Leth-Chain: This Holy Mountain should only be attempted during the summer months. At 3,470 feet in the Cairngorm Mountain Range, about three miles north of the Ben MacDhui summit and overlooking the Lairig-Grhu, this mountain presents a long hike, depending upon the route taken. The best approach is to take the ski-lift to the summit of Cairn Gorm from where it is a relatively easy walk down a ridge to the Charged Rock.

Remember that nearby Ben MacDhui is now a Retreat of The Great White Brotherhood!

Old Man, Coniston: Overlooking Coniston Water in the Lake District of northern England, the Old Man, at 2,635 feet, presents a two-hours' hard climb. Can be climbed year-round. Attempt only during the summer months unless under supervision of an experienced Aetherius Society guide. Rain and mist can loom up without warning. Shortest approach is from the quarry, road conditions permitting.

Pen-Y-Fan: At 2,906 feet in the Brecon Beacons of South Wales, this Holy Mountain has very severe winter conditions, with bad weather possible at any time of the year. Attempt only during the summer months. Approach from the village of Brecon. The route leads through a former small-arms military firing range which is no longer in operation. The Brecon Beacons and Pen-Y-Fan remain a primary winter training area for Britain's elite S.A.S. due to the severity of its weather. Allow several hours to climb this mountain.

Carnedd Llywelyn: Best approach to the 3,485-foot peak is from the south via the main A5 road between Llyn Ogwen and Capel Curig. There is a fairly easy circular ridge walk, or a steep, straight climb from Llyn Ogwen via Carnedd Dafwdd. Snow conditions in winter can be among the worst in the British Isles. Heavy mists frequently come down without warning. The climb should be made only during the summer months, unless very well equipped and accompanied by an experienced Aetherius Society guide.

Kinderscout: At 2,080 feet, this is the highest peak in the Peak District of Derbyshire. Approaching from Hayfield, it presents a long, hard climb, and should only be attempted in optimum, non-frosty weather conditions. All pilgrims must be careful to stay on the mountain trail.

Yes Tor: Situated on treacherous Dartmoor, this 2,030-foot Holy Mountain presents a two-hour climb, but not a steep one, from the town of Oakhampton. Marshes may be a problem and thick fogs can descend without warning. Consult the table of firing practice of high-explosive artillery posted in Oakhampton concerning the military firing range in this area, which is operative all year round with the exception of August and most weekends. Oakhampton Police will provide this information by telephone. It is possible to drive to within a 30-minute hike of the Charged Rock, but this should be done only if required by age or physical condition.

The United States of America

Mount Baldy: A very popular summer hiking and winter skiing area, 50 miles north-east of Los Angeles, California, near the borders of the Angeles and San Bernardino National Forests. Use Mountain Avenue north from Interstate 10 at Ontario and drive through Baldy Village to the bottom of the year-round ski-lift at over 6,000 feet. The last few miles of this road are very steep, winding, and at high altitude, which requires an automobile in good condition. Take the ski-lift to the 7,800-foot lodge in Baldy Notch. The climb to the Charged Rock at 9,552 feet takes about two-and-a-half hours. The Charged Spot is below the main peak, up a steep slope of loose scree. Air is thin due to altitude and the Sun's intensity demands headwear. Summer temperatures can be hot and water should be carried. Strong footgear, an absiel sling with carabiner should be worn, and several members of the party should have climbing rope in the event of a fall on some very steep portions of this climb. Pilgrims should attempt this Holy Mountain only between June and early October, and then only in good weather. Southern California is drought-prone, but heavy rain and snowfall can change the characteristics of this mountain from year to year. Has been climbed throughout the winter by experienced Aetherius Society climbers with full arctic climbing gear, but this is not recommended! Winds to 70 miles per hour, severe avalanche hazard, deep snow and ice are present. Permission to climb in winter must be obtained from National Forest Service Rangers in Baldy Village who will inspect equipment and question climbers' experience.

(For text of a Transmission describing the Energy in Mount Baldy, see Chapter 4.)

Mount Tallac: At 9,735 feet, the Charged Spot looks down over Fallen Leaf Lake to the south, and the giant Lake Tahoe to the north-east. The first step is to get to South Lake Tahoe at 7,000 feet in the Sierra Nevada Mountains. From there, three approaches are recommended. Perhaps the easiest is from Camp Richardson on Highway 89 on Lake Tahoe's south-west shoreline. Pack horses and mules can be rented here for an extended stay at the high meadow. The trail is well marked. Two other approaches are via Fallen Leaf Lake, both starting from Fallen Leaf Lodge, about 10 miles south off Highway 89. The original route of the Team was along the west shore of Fallen Leaf Lake for several miles, then to Pyramid Lake and up the steep slope to a high meadow. The third approach is from the Lodge into the Desolation Wilderness area, then back up to the high meadow. The Charged Rock is only about 200 yards from the meadow. High altitude, intense sunlight and possible heavy rain must be anticipated in summer. Climbing months are between June and October. This is a four-hour climb from lake level for persons in good physical condition, who should carry water and food, and should wear strong footgear (mountain boots preferred) due to the roughness of the terrain. From a packed-in camp at Pyramid Lake, the Charged Rock can be reached in a vigorous one-and-a-half hours. This is an ideal opportunity for outdoors types to make multiple easy pilgrimages, surrounded by the stunning beauty of tall pine forests. Conditions are very severe in winter and access is then restricted by National Forest Service Rangers.

(For text of a Mental Contact from the Master Jesus on Mount Tallac, see Chapter 4.)

Mount Adams: This Holy Mountain, 5,798 feet in the Presidential Range of the White Mountains in New Hampshire, is frequently climbed by pilgrims of The Aetherius Society from our Detroit, Michigan Branch, and Toronto, Canada Group, who are very familiar and well-informed from personal experience. Having said that, we must give a few words of warning. All the mountains of the Presidential Range are reliably reputed to have some of the worst weather in America. Winds in excess of 243 miles per hour have been recorded there — the highest ever recorded on Earth outside of a tornado or hurricane! Climbers must realize that, despite its comparatively low elevation for America, this Range MUST BE RESPECTED! Winter-type mountaineering clothing and equipment, as well as good rain gear, should be carried at all times of the year!

Pilgrims should approach through Gorham on State Route 2. They should contact The Appalachian Mountain Club nearby on Route 16 concerning current weather conditions and forecasts, and to confirm previously made reservations at the Madison Hut, about three to five-and-a-half hours climb, depending upon weather and climbers' condition. The Madison Hut is usually fully booked and reservations should be made several months in advance. During its season — from Memorial Day weekend until Labor Day weekend — the Madison Hut is fully staffed and stocked by Club employees. Sleeping accommodations and meals are available for a charge here. Frequent climbers recommend early July to early August as the best times to climb Mount Adams.

Probably the best trail is the Valley Way Trail from below, north of Mount Adams on Route 2, to the Madison Hut. This is the trail used by the Club. The Madison Hut is about 1,000 feet below the peak, and just above the tree line at 4,300 feet. At least one hour over very difficult terrain is required after leaving the hut. The Gulfside Trail to Lowes Path to the summit is the longer and easier trail from the hut, but Airline Trail, which is shorter, may also be used. Check first with the Club and follow their advice!

For a package of information on the White Mountains, the Madison Hut, maps of Mount Adams, etc., contact:

The Appalachian Mountain Club
P.O. Box 298
Route 16
Gorham, NH 03581
Or call: (603) 466-2721
For reservations call: (603) 466-2727

(For text of a Mental Contact made on Mount Adams by Mars Sector 6, see Chapter 4.)

Castle Peak: Due to its elevation of 14,259 feet in Colorado's Rocky Mountains, this Holy Mountain also has special requirements. Arriving in Aspen, near 8,000 feet, pilgrims should allow time to acclimatize to the rarified atmosphere. At least several days, with exercise, should be allowed, and a week would be even better. High altitude sun-blockers are locally available in this extremely popular area. Buy the best and be sure to demand a product for protection at 14,000 feet, not the lower elevations around Aspen where hiking and fishing are favourite pastimes. Several excellent campgrounds are nearby. This Holy Mountain should only be attempted between June and September. Blizzards have been experienced on the peak by pilgrims in August, although these were of short duration. Seek local advice and follow it! Either hire a guide or, if you are an experienced driver, hire a Jeep-type vehicle locally.

Start just after sunrise and allow all the hours of daylight for a round-trip. Weather conditions and driving expertise permitting, you can drive from Aspen, through Castle Creek Valley, past the tree line at 11,000 feet to the Montezuma Mine. Roads above the tree line are poorly, if at all, maintained and you must use 4-wheel drive at very low speed in a low gear for safety. There will be washouts and other hazards, and near the Montezuma Mine, a permanent glacier will eventually stop you completely. You MUST NOT attempt to cross this in a vehicle! Once above the tree line, be prepared to STOP and park your vehicle as conditions require, and hike from there!

From the Montezuma Mine, the Charged Rock is about a

one-hour hike, with the last half-hour up a steep slope of loose scree which requires caution. You should be equipped with full mountain-climbing gear and clothing, carrying extra food and water. You may have to start your climb from the tree line, which would add another hour at least. Be prepared for everything, including a sudden change in weather.

Remember that Castle Peak is a Retreat of The Great White Brotherhood and conduct yourself accordingly!

(For text of the Special Commendation given to the Castle Peak Team, see Chapter 4.)

Australia

Mount Kosciusko: At 7,314 feet in the Snowy Mountain Range of New South Wales, this is Australia's highest point of land. From Canberra, the national Capital, drive south to the eastern side of the Snowy Mountains area. A special permit may be required from the Snowy Mountain Hydro-Electric Authority to drive in this area, at your own risk, due to road and climate conditions. Arriving in Jyndabine, check with locals for road conditions and directions to approach the mountain more closely. Try for the Cooinda Motel or other accommodation about seven miles west in Wilson's Valley. There **may be** a road open directly to the summit from there. Remember that Australia is in the Southern Hemisphere, where the seasons are reversed from the Northern Hemisphere. Southern summer is the equivalent of northern winter! Be sure to check beforehand with an Australian Consulate or Tourist Bureau for climatic conditions before you leave home. Carry clothing and equipment appropriate for the climb. Expect a climb of about four hours at most, depending upon where you leave your vehicle. Rain, mist or low cloud may obscure your vision, but the climb is not really steep until the last mile. In local winter, expect snow and more difficult conditions, and probably a longer hike

(For text of the Mental Contact by the Master Aetherius on Mount Kosciusko, see Chapter 4.)

Mount Ramshead: At 7,197 feet in the same range of mountains, Mount Ramshead is only five miles south of Mount Kosciusko, but on the opposite or western side in an area called the Ramshead Range. The approach is from Thredbo from where a ski-lift takes you high into this range. The climb to the Charged Spot takes about three hours through gentle terrain. The Charged Rock is about 100 yards farther on, a gigantic, almost square block of granite, with a flat top which can easily seat a dozen people. Another huge rock points directly at the Charged Spot, making it fairly easy to locate. In local summer, this is quite an easy and very pleasant climb, though pilgrims should, as always, be prepared for inclement weather.

(For text of the Mental Contact from Mars Sector 6 on Mount Ramshead, see Chapter 4.)

New Zealand

Mount Wakefield: Located on the larger, but less populous South Island, Mount Wakefield is in the Southern Alps region near the western coast. The approach, however, is from the east. Pilgrims can fly to the base of Mount Wakefield, or go by car or bus from Christchurch, two-and-a-half hours to Mount Cook Village. Accommodations are at the Hermitage Hotel and Chalets, the Glencoe Lodge Motel, and a small campground. Mount Cook is the major peak in the range and Mount Wakefield, at 6,651 feet, is visible nearby from the "Hermitage." This is a difficult climb, very steep at times over rough terrain cut by deep valleys and surrounded by the permanent Tasman Glacier. Local guides, or the New Zealand Branch of The Aetherius Society in Auckland, can advise pilgrims of the only safe route which, depending upon extremely changeable weather and physical conditions, can require more than nine hours for a round-trip. Full mountain equipment and emergency rations with plenty of water are essential.

Climbable from October to April/May with good boots and wet weather gear, Mount Wakefield should only be climbed in local winter, from May to September, by experienced climbers. Guides and gear are hireable from the Alpine Guide Shop. Park Rangers provide daily forecasts and climbing conditions, and maintain a "sign in" book for all climbers.

(For text of the Mental Contact with the Master Jesus on Mount Wakefield, see Chapter 4.)

Africa

Mount Kilimanjaro: Rising to 19,335 feet in Tanzania, East Africa, Mount Kilimanjaro is the highest peak in Africa. As such, it is frequently climbed or partially climbed by mountaineers and tourists. Outward Bound maintains climbing schools in the area and has built shelters along the climbing route. The Tanzania High Commission in other countries will assist with travel arrangements, route, hiring of guides and porters. Monsoon seasons are generally around April-May and October-November and should be avoided.

Mount Kilimanjaro is now climbed from the Tanzania side only. There is a Mount Kilimanjaro International Airport near the town of Moshi. From there, regular buses run to Marangu Hotel, which is the base camp for climbs to the peak. There are large airports also in Nairobi and Mombasa, Kenya, from which pilgrims can drive to Moshi.

This Holy Mountain consists of three peaks, the centre and highest called Kibo or, more recently Uhuru, is accepted by The Aetherius Society to be the location of the Charged Spot. This will require five days — three days up and two days down — with overnight stops at various caves and huts leading to Gillman's Point, just below the peak. Porters will generally not climb past the Kibo Hut (or School Hut) at 15,300 feet, which is the final overnight stop before the summit. Climbers will very likely be in intense cold, extremely exposed to the elements, under very intense sunlight and in extremely rarified air. Their age, physical condition and pre-climb exercise and endurance will all be major factors in a successful pilgrimage. Full expedition-type mountain gear and clothing, together with ample food and water, are essential.

Since this climb can be virtually "laid on" as an organized safari by the government and the Marangu Hotel, further instructions will not be given here as these may change from time to time.

Always remember that Mount Kilimanjaro is a Retreat of The Great White Brotherhood!

Europe

For the remaining two Holy Mountains, we can do no better than to quote our Master's own instructions printed in *Cosmic Voice,* Issue No. 25, November-December 1961.

Mount Madrigerfluh: 8,770 feet in the Swiss Alps near Davos.

"Proceed from Davos up the Schatzalpan mountain train. Then take the gondola lift to the Strella Pass. From the top, follow the exit sign to the outside of the station where you will find a path leading to the left. After about a 20-minute hike, you will come to a small lake which you pass on your right side. Keep to the lower path after the lake towards the floor of the valley, where you will come to a signpost. Madrigerfluh is in front of you and slightly to your right, but is a very long way away. It is climbable from here, but we do not advise it. It is better to turn left at this signpost in the valley and proceed up a steep path, keeping a mountain called Korbshorn on your right. Keep to the lower path and after about an hour and a half, you will come to the Korbshorn Hut where you may rest. Madrigerfluh rises from the floor at the far end of the valley, almost like a huge pyramid.

"Leaving the hut, you lose height and go down toward the valley floor part way, keeping the Korbshorn ridge on the right. Eventually you will come to the foot of Madrigerfluh, with a very steep climb ahead of you. At this stage, bear right and ascend the ridge in a zig-zag fashion where it is less steep. You will come to a flagpole on a lower peak, but this is not the Charged Rock. Proceed along the ridge toward the summit until you come to a rocky wall in front of you, which you bypass by descending a little and then climbing upward again. At the end of this climb, there is a rocky bowl surrounded by boulders, looking rather like an upturned saucer. Proceed straight across, where the summit can be gained. The summit itself is a rounded grassy peak. This is the Charged Place."

Le Nid d'Aigle: "The point Charged was a huge rocky ledge, approximately 8,700 feet in elevation, overlooking the Chamonix Valley in the Mont Blanc area of France. This ledge is unnamed on maps, but by carefully following these instructions, it should be easy for any pilgrims to find their way there.

"First proceed to Les Houches, a small village three miles west of Chamonix. Here take the ski-lift to Bellevue, and from there take a mountain train which will bring you to the terminus of Le Nid d'Aigle.

"From this terminus, a path will lead towards Mont Blanc, the Glacier de Bionassay and the Refuge de la Tete Rousse. A few yards along this path is a sign pointing to the Refuge de la Tete Rousse on the left. Follow this steep rocky path until you come to a broken-down hut, directly in your path. Standing with the doorway at your back, you will see, on your immediate left, two rocky masses overlooking the valley of Chamonix. If you then proceed over a deep ridge to the direct left of the path to Tete Rousse hut, passing the first rocky pinnacle on your left, you will come to the second rocky pinnacle which is the highest one directly overlooking the valley. When you come to the bottom of this, you will see two peaks. Climb up between these two peaks. When you come up the depression between them, you will see the Symbol of The Aetherius Society on the left hand peak. This is the Charged Rock.

"From the train terminus it will take about two-and-a-half hours to reach the Holy Rock. This pilgrimage can easily be made in one day from Les Houches."

We are indebted to our Master for these instructions. Please bear in mind that these words were written in 1961 and some conditions may have changed since then. Climbers must observe all the precautions regarding mountain gear and clothing, food and water, and climbing seasons so often repeated in this Chapter.

* * * * * * * * * * * * * * *

In closing this Guide For Pilgrimages, there are a few general observations which should be made.

1. **Lightning.** At high altitudes, especially in barren places, YOU are likely to be the tallest object in your vicinity! If you see the beginnings of an electrical storm, get several yards away from your pack (which probably contains metal) and lie flat on the ground until the storm passes.

2. **Conduct.** You are in a Holy Place and should conduct yourself accordingly, with the respect and reverence which you would show in a Church, Temple or other Sacred structure. Do not litter. Pack up all trash. Follow the U.S. Park Service advice: "Take nothing but pictures; leave nothing but footprints."

3. **Karma.** Although all of the Holy Mountains are now interlinked and freely exchange their specific Energies, the Law of Karma **always** recognizes **effort!** Taking into consideration your age, physical condition, weather and terrain conditions, your climbing experience and the welfare of those with you, make your **best effort** at all times to climb as close as possible to the Charged Spot. This will increase the benefit of your pilgrimage, not only to yourself, but to the world as a whole! But do not unnecessarily risk yourself or others, including possible rescue teams, by climbing beyond your resources or the demands of conditions. Karma does not reward the foolhardy, especially where they risk others than themselves.

A PILGRIMAGE ON MOUNT BALDY

On Mount Baldy in Southern California, 52 people climbed with our Master to the nearly 10,000-foot Charged Spot to contact and radiate powerful Spiritual Energies to the world in July 1960. This spot was used in 1966 by a smaller, more specialized Team to inaugurate **Operation Sunbeam,** a Mission in which the Energies of the Holy Mountains — placed there for the benefit of mankind — are directed instead to The Logos Of Earth. This is the most potent Karmic manipulation taking place upon the Planet today!

THE HOLY CROSSES

CHAPTER 9

THE HOLY CROSSES

His Eminence Sir George King, using Holy Stones collected by Members of The Aetherius Society from each of the 19 Holy Mountains of the world, created an unique and powerful Holy Cross which was unveiled and Consecrated during a Sacred Ceremony at the American Headquarters of The Aetherius Society in Hollywood, California, on February 1st, 1981.

There now exist three of these wonderful radiators of Spiritual Energy in the world. The second was installed in the European Headquarters in London, England, on January 23rd, 1982; and the third Holy Cross was installed in the Northern Headquarters in Barnsley, England, on October 1st, 1989.

All three of these magnificent Holy Crosses were hand-made entirely by Members of The Aetherius Society, including the precision woodworking, gilding and lacquering; the core-drilling, cabachoning and polishing of the Holy Stones; and the gold-plated Sterling Silver mountings surrounding each stone.

On February 1st, 1981, during the Dedication Ceremony in Hollywood, the following Address prepared by His Eminence was read out to the congregation by Dr. Charles Abrahamson:

> "The Cross which now stands in Glory upon our Altar, is complete.
>
> "The mystic and most ancient Symbols atop thereof stand for: *The manifestation of Almighty God as Wisdom.* Thus the Symbology in the Shape Power of the Holy Cross depicts: ***Resurrection into God's Wisdom.***
>
> "On the body and arms of this Holy Cross are set 19 Charged Stones from 19 Holy Mountains throughout the world. They are placed with insight and knowledge which is only possessed by a Master of great experience. This makes the Symbolism a perfect balance, in that the Cosmic

Energies from these Stones add a supporting power to its very essence.

"This Holy Cross, as a whole, is more complete than any other known Symbol of its kind on the surface of the Planet Earth.

"His Eminence Sir George King, who designed this Holy Cross and worked out the correct placement of the Charged Stones — strategically complementing each other's intermingling Spiritual Energies — has, by his own statement, this morning performed but a preliminary Blessing of this Holy Cross. Being the Master that he is, he will continue further Blessing in a mystic ritual which other eyes may not, at this time, look upon.

"Our hearts leap with joyous praise for being allowed such a truly Holy Cross in our Temple, and we now must thank Almighty God for the Wisdom He has bestowed upon a true Spiritual Disciple, namely, His Eminence Sir George King, Metropolitan Archbishop of The Aetherius Churches.

"His Eminence has commanded us all to spend some time daily in Prayer for the next seven days. This Prayer should be one of thankfulness to Almighty God for being able to have upon our little Altar such a powerful, Holy Symbol of Enlightenment and Advancement, as this complete Holy Cross."

A CONTEMPLATION

When you gaze upon this Cross, think of Those Whose radiant Emanations are behind its Jewels:

LORDS OF KARMA!
THE MASTER AETHERIUS!
MARS SECTOR 8 AND
CLOSE COSMIC ASSOCIATES!

THE MASTER MARS SECTOR 6!
THE MASTER JESUS!
SAINT GOO-LING!
PRIMARY TERRESTRIAL MENTAL CHANNEL!

THE COSMIC ADEPTS — THE FULL ASPECTS OF NIXIES ZERO ZERO ONE, NIXIES ZERO ZERO TWO AND NIXIES ZERO ZERO THREE!

TWO CHOSEN HIGH-RANKING MEMBERS OF THE SUPREME COUNCIL OF THE SPIRITUAL HIERARCHY OF EARTH!

HOLY CROSS SEMINAR BY HIS EMINENCE

On February 15th, 1981, during a Seminar on the Holy Cross, His Eminence imparted the following Wisdom regarding the design of these magnificent Holy Crosses:

HIS EMINENCE SIR GEORGE KING:

We have 19 Holy Mountains throughout the world, each one Charged by one of The Cosmic Masters. Eighteen of these Holy Mountains were Charged through myself — as a channel only. The Power was certainly not mine; it came from a much, much higher Source than myself, from People hundreds of thousands of lives ahead of the body that was presented on those Mountains. Neither did all the Spiritual Energy put into these Mountains come through my body — but just a small portion of it.

Last year I designed a special Cross in which stones from all these Holy Mountains could appear. We were very fortunate in that Members making pilgrimages to these 19 mountains in the past had collected stones for us. My idea of the Cross in our Temple is that it had to have stones from all 19 of the Holy Mountains in its body.

A Cross Shape itself is not complete; according to one of the great Founders of the Christian Church:

> *"It is not complete unless atop thereof is affixed the Holy Symbol."*

This information was given to us many years ago by no less a Person than the Apostle Saint Peter. He even went further and Charged such a Cross after we had manufactured it. This small Cross has been in England for many years now and the emanations from it are as strong today as the time it was originally Charged.

So therefore, it had to be complete, and to make it complete we had to affix to the top of the Cross the Symbol under which The Aetherius Society was founded. As you know, these Symbols are probably the most ancient in the world: one of them is the ancient Symbol for God, and the other is the very ancient Symbol of Wisdom. When placed together, they mean:

"God manifesting Itself as Wisdom."

My Cross had to go further than even that. It had to have its Spiritual Power really complete. So therefore, one sure way of guaranteeing this was to incorporate into the body and arms of that Cross, 19 Holy Stones taken from the 19 Holy Mountains throughout the world.

This is where the expertise had to come in. It was not a matter of placing those stones anywhere on the Cross. They had to be positioned precisely in the best possible balanced positions on the body of the Cross.

To balance the design of such a Cross you have to first consider the four major points — the top, the middle of the Cross arms, and the end of each arm. Those are the major points of balance in any Cross in the world. In order to bring about a major balance, and then go into a minor balancing as well, I drew upon my own personal experience of these Holy Mountains, as well as information from Higher Sources.

Looking at the diagram of this Holy Cross you can see that the centre holds the stone from one of the Holiest spots on Earth — Carnedd Llywelyn — and that the other three major positions all hold stones from mountains with special Powers: Mount Kilimanjaro, Castle Peak and Ben Hope.

Adding Brown Willy and Le Nid d'Aigle to the upper part gave great Spiritual Power at the top of the Cross. Also, I felt that the whole top of the Cross would then provide a balancing aspect to the Power from the Symbol on the top, which is radionically connected to the rest of the Cross.

Holdstone Down and Mount Tallac are positioned on either side of the centre; they are both very powerful mountains and were both Charged by the Master Jesus in Operation Starlight.

All of the stones in any of the upper positions are from mountains which are powerful. Notice the position of Mount Adams, which contains great Healing Energies.

All stones below Mount Baldy are relatively mild in their influence, with the exception of Mount Ramshead. Mount Ramshead, therefore, prevents too much of a Power drop towards the bottom of the Cross. So we have a Cross which has been deliberately designed to be extremely powerful at the top, especially at the four major points, and then to have a relative fade-off of Power towards the bottom.

This Cross is an intense Spiritual Power generator. Note that, as with any Cross, because of its Shape Power, the main intersecting lines of Power are at 45 degrees to the centre of the Cross. There may be 20,000 - 30,000 beams of Spiritual Energy radiating away, all at approximately 45 degree angles to the centre of this Cross.

With the careful design and exact proportions, together with the capping of the top of the Cross with two Holy Symbols acting in harmony and balance, plus the fact that 19 Charged Stones from the Holy Mountains of the world are incorporated in this carefully designed Shape Power, makes this into an intense Spiritual Energy Radiator. No matter how often this is used, or how much Energy either radiates from it naturally or is drawn from it by mystical ritual, the Power in this Cross will never be exhausted. Every stone has an unbreakable link with its source, and the more Energy drawn through every stone, the more that stone — acting as a natural receiver — will draw from its source.

The Cross, now placed with deference upon the Altar, will radiate its beautiful Spiritual Energies to all people who enter our Temple. The more Spiritual they are, the more they will receive. The better their motive when they come here to give thanks and offer Prayers, the better help they will receive, from a Spiritual point of view, from this beautiful, yet fully operative device.

I have given you a Cross here which is not only unique in its design and that which it supports, but which is a powerful radiator of the truly magnificent blend of Spiritual Energies originally put into the Holy Mountains by The Cosmic Masters.

I now declare the design of this Cross to be a present to mankind in celebration of my 62nd birthday.

We have in our Cross a work of metaphysical art which is, at the same time, a most practical and most Sacred religious masterpiece.

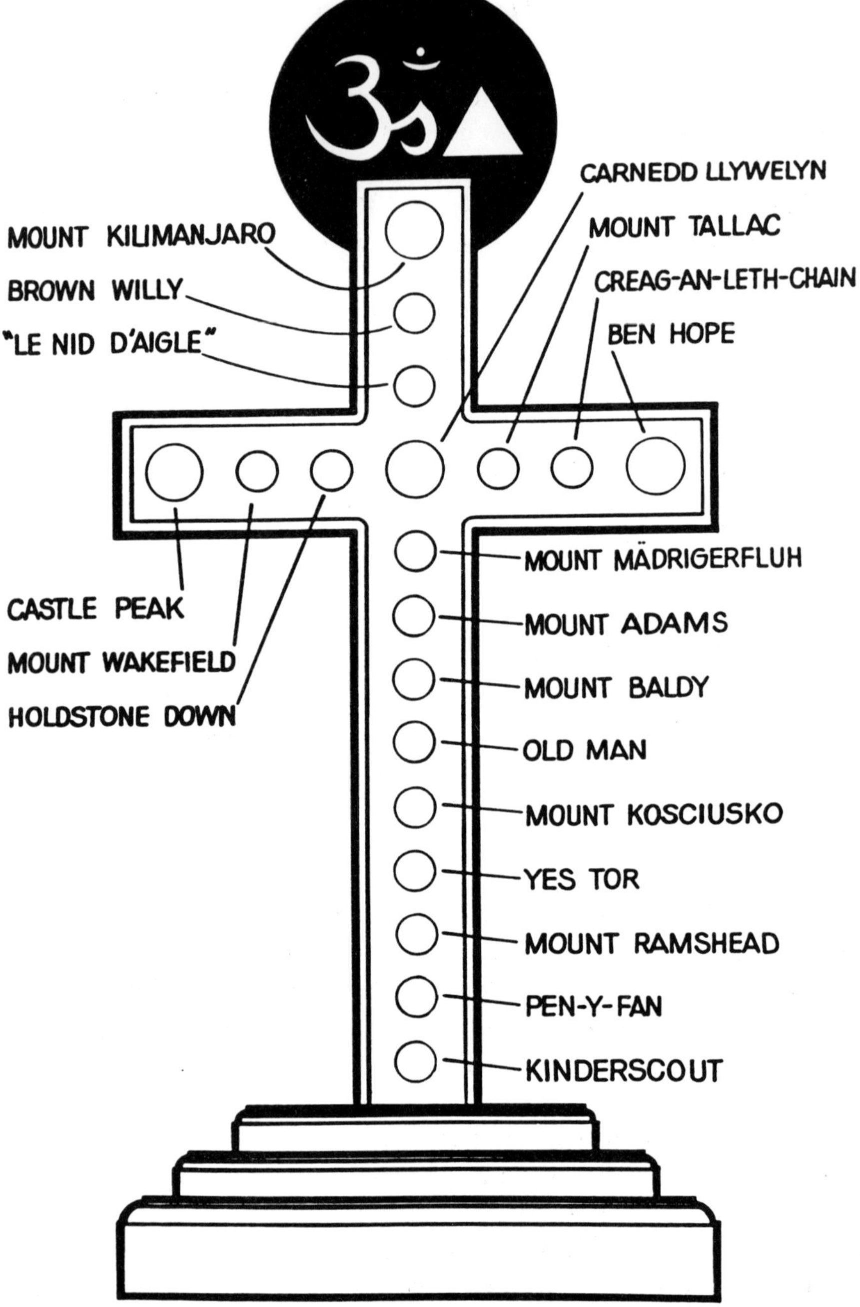
CARNEDD LLYWELYN
MOUNT TALLAC
CREAG-AN-LETH-CHAIN
BEN HOPE
MOUNT KILIMANJARO
BROWN WILLY
"LE NID D'AIGLE"
CASTLE PEAK
MOUNT WAKEFIELD
HOLDSTONE DOWN
MOUNT MÄDRIGERFLUH
MOUNT ADAMS
MOUNT BALDY
OLD MAN
MOUNT KOSCIUSKO
YES TOR
MOUNT RAMSHEAD
PEN-Y-FAN
KINDERSCOUT

CHAPTER 10

OUR HOLY CROSS SEEN THROUGHOUT THE GALAXY

On October 5th, 1993, while he was in his Santa Barbara residence, Our Master was in Mental Contact with the Master Aetherius for approximately one full hour. The original purpose of establishing this Contact was to obtain, if possible, information needed for this book.

On our Master's desk during this Mental Contact was a copy of *Cosmic Voice,* Volume 2, Issues 2 and 3, February 1981 — a Special Edition dedicated to the Holy Cross which is reprinted in part in the beginning of this Chapter. The Master Aetherius noticed this Issue and after He had given His Eminence the information he was seeking, this Great Cosmic Master opened the following dialogue:

The Master Aetherius: "Now, can you do me a favour?"

His Eminence: "Anything You like."

The Master Aetherius: "That 'Cosmic Voice' which you have been reading just lately, with the Holy Cross on the cover — if you could just put out the drawing of the Cross and tell me when I can scan that."

His Eminence: "Oh, we will do that right now if You wish."

The Master Aetherius: "That would be very good."

His Eminence: "Just that drawing with all the names of the mountains on — is that it?"

The Master Aetherius: "Yes, that will do fine."

His Eminence: "And how about the picture on the front?"

The Master Aetherius: "And that too."

His Eminence: "Thank You very much, Master Aetherius. We will do that now. We will spread it out flat on a table and I will let You know when."

The Master Aetherius: "Thank you very much. Aetherius now out."

His Eminence: "This is His Eminence, now out."

(There was a short pause while His Eminence's aides in Santa Barbara made the preparations, and placed the pages indicated on a table outside the house.)

His Eminence: "I will now move away. Will that be good enough for You?"

The Master Aetherius: "Absolutely great, thank you. I will let you know when I am finished."

His Eminence: "There are no people on that side of the house at all, and the nearest person to You is myself. Is that all right?"

The Master Aetherius: "Yes, fine."

His Eminence: "Thank You."

The Master Aetherius: "Yes, I have moved in for one picture. I will take one or two more."

(The Master Aetherius was in a Spacecraft in close orbit of Earth at the time.)

His Eminence: "Where will this scan go?"

The Master Aetherius: "Oh, I would say **to the far ends of the Galaxy!"**

His Eminence: "Good Lord, really? I will arrange for You to make a scan of the original article when I arrive back in Los Angeles, if You would like that?"

The Master Aetherius: "I would deeply appreciate that."

His Eminence: "Very well, I will do that — or even before. Where would You need the Cross placed — outside?"

The Master Aetherius: "No, on a table in the middle of the Temple would do very well."

His Eminence: "Very well. So that can be done, when can You scan it?"

The Master Aetherius: "You arrange it and I will let you know."

His Eminence: "Thank You very much. So just standing on a table on its base in the middle of the Temple?"

The Master Aetherius: "Yes, definitely."

His Eminence: "About where we put the **Operation Sunbeam** equipment?"

The Master Aetherius: "Perfect."

His Eminence: "Thank You very much."

The Master Aetherius: "I have taken a picture of these and thank you very much."

His Eminence: "I will let You know when the Holy Cross is in position, Master Aetherius. This is His Eminence, now out."

The Master Aetherius: "Master Aetherius, now out."

(There was another pause while the Holy Cross was placed in position in the Temple in Los Angeles.)

His Eminence: "This is His Eminence to the Master Aetherius. That has not taken us very long. The Temple in Los Angeles has been cleared and the Holy Cross has been placed roughly where we put the instrumentation for **Operation Sunbeam.** It is all ready for You. The building is now empty."

The Master Aetherius: "Thank you very much."

His Eminence: "Will You let me know when You are finished?"

The Master Aetherius: "Certainly."

His Eminence: "Thank You very much, Master Aetherius. This is His Eminence standing by."

(There was a further short pause while the scan was made.)

His Eminence: "Yes, Master Aetherius. You have done it? The whole thing has taken less than an hour from the start of the Transmission until now. Very well!"

The Master Aetherius: "I deeply appreciate it and thank those who helped in this 'set-up,' I believe you would call it, for me this morning."

His Eminence: "Thank You very much; I will do that."

The Master Aetherius: "This is Aetherius, now out."

His Eminence: "This is His Eminence, now out. The time is now 11:24 on October the 5th. Much has happened here this morning!"

* * * * * * * * * * *

This information, published here for the first time, has been given to only a handful of people. We thank His Eminence for allowing us this exclusive "scoop!"

CHAPTER 11

HOLY STONE SHAPES

In 1975, His Eminence took a further step forward in Operation Starlight. Since it is not possible for most pilgrims to visit the mountains as often as they would like — if even at all — certain of the Holy Mountains have been brought to the pilgrims as a sparkling piece of polished rock set into a suitable, radionically-designed wooden shape.

The first Holy Stone to be used in this new revolutionary project was, naturally enough, Holdstone Down. Following a pilgrimage to this Charged Mountain, rocks were gathered which could be suitably cut into workable slabs by a professional lapidary. From these slabs, small stones were core-drilled and cabochoned by Aetherius Society Staff before being set into delicately-crafted wooden Crosses. This ancient Symbol had been described by the Master Jesus in "The Twelve Blessings" as **"the lasting Symbol of Resurrection of the Spirit of Man, up to the Mighty Godhead — through Karmic experience."** Let us not forget, in considering His Eminence's choice of this particular Shape, that it was, of course, the Master Jesus Who had provided the Charge for Holdstone Down, thus making this radionic instrument metaphysically balanced in every way, and therefore extremely powerful.

This inspired project now also includes Shapes containing stones from two of the American Charged Mountains, Mount Baldy and Mount Adams, each of which is set into exactly proportioned triangles; and Mount Kosciusko in Australia, with the cabochoned stone being mounted onto a circle. A fifth Shape contains a Holy Stone from the Creag-An-Leth-Chain, set into a wooden arch-like structure and supported by a 24-karat gold-plated creation, symbolizing the "Torch of Light" fueling the "Flame of Consciousness." This highly inspirational Shape not only demonstrates His Eminence's advanced understanding of the science of Shape Power but also incorporates the knowledge that this Holy Mountain Range is now a Retreat of The Great White Brotherhood!

A sixth Shape manufactured by The Aetherius Society is from another of the Charged Mountains of North America, set into a maple wood Cross. Additional Holy Stone Shapes will be released in the future.

As wonderfully valuable and practical as these Holy artifacts are to their owners, they cannot, of course, substitute for an actual pilgrimage to the Holy Mountains. As this book has explained, all New Age pilgrims who visit any of the Holy Mountains of the world with a pure, unselfish motive, are able to invoke tremendous Spiritual Energies which are then radiated outwards by the Devic Forces for the benefit of all mankind. The Holy Stone Shapes, however, being radionically linked to their parent mountain and thereby all of the Holy Mountains of the world, provide Spiritual, inspirational and healing benefits to the user in their Spiritual work. These benefits should never be undervalued and to most people, their Holy Stone Shapes are among their most prized possessions.

The value takes on even more of a priceless sense for all those who have requested to have their Shapes Blessed. This is an unique Service which, yet again, His Eminence has undertaken for our benefit. Using his very advanced metaphysical and occult knowledge, he Blesses each Shape with a Blessing personal to the owner. As if this were not enough, the Creag-An-Leth-Chain Shape is given a second Blessing by a Member of The Great White Brotherhood!

It is through these Holy Stone Shapes that New Age seekers can bring the tremendous Spiritual emanations of the mountains Charged in Operation Starlight into their own homes and daily lives. Most owners place their Shapes on small altars within their homes from where they can perform Spiritual practices for their own personal well-being and advancement, as well as to radiate Prayer Energy out to the world as a whole. It is in such an environment and for such purposes that the Holy Stone Shapes are ideally suited; for just as with the mountains themselves, the Shapes respond to our Spiritual practices and invocation, becoming increasingly active and powerful the more we tune in to their sacred emanations.

EPILOGUE

"Bid the pilgrims to come hither......."

The Master Jesus — after Charging two of
The Holy Mountains Of The World